10789

For Reference

Not to be taken from this room

LIBRARY
ST. MICHAEL'S PREP SCHOOL
1042 STAR RT. - ORANGE, CA. 92667

D1773467

Eyewitness Accounts of the American Revolution

Journal of Captain Pausch

Edited by William L. Stone

The New York Times & Arno Press

Reprint Edition 1971 by Arno Press Inc.

*

LC# 79-140876
ISBN 0-405-01200-4

*

Eyewitness Accounts of the American Revolution, Series III
ISBN for complete set: 0-405-01187-3

*

Manufactured in the United States of America

JOURNAL
OF
CAPTAIN PAUSCH

Myladum Vrinnum de Riedesel née de Massow

JOURNAL

OF

CAPTAIN PAUSCH

CHIEF OF THE HANAU ARTILLERY DURING THE

BURGOYNE CAMPAIGN.

TRANSLATED AND ANNOTATED

BY

WILLIAM L. STONE.

Introduction by

EDWARD J. LOWELL.

ALBANY, N. Y.
JOEL MUNSELL'S SONS, 82 STATE ST.
M.DCCC.LXXXVI.

TO

General Horatio Rogers,

Whose admirable editorship of Hadden's
Journal, justly entitles him to rank as
one of the most accomplished of
Burgoyne's scholars, this volume
is affectionately dedicated by
his old college-mate,
the Translator.

PREFACE.

THERE are two ways of translating. One is to paraphase the original: the other is to give the text literally. The first method admits of an elegant rendering, by which the different shades of an author's meaning are often sacrificed to beauty of diction. The second, at the expense of style, aims to give clearly the writer's ideas. This last is the plan I have adopted in this translation, believing that the reader would prefer to know just what Pausch intended to convey.

The translation of this Journal has been attended with peculiar difficulties, from the fact that much of it is in language now obsolete. Especially is this the case in regard to technical terms used to describe military manœuvres. Fortunately, however, I have had the aid of several gentlemen who have served for a long time in

PREFACE

the Prussian army, one of whom, being a native of Hesse-Hanau, is specially familiar with the idioms of the language in that part of Germany. Thus, my thanks are particularly due to Mr. Henry A. Fischer, of New York City, Mr. Robert Moeller of Jersey City, Mr. Eugene Vogel of New York City, formerly an officer in the 9th Regiment of the Schleswig Holstein Field-Artillery, and also to Dr. James A. Butler of Madison, Wis. — himself an accomplished German scholar — for valuable aid in unravelling several knotty passages. I am also under heavy obligation to Mr. Edward J. Lowell, for giving my readers the benefit of his great store of knowledge regarding the relations existing, at the time that Pausch wrote, between the English Government and the petty German Princes; and likewise to Mr. Wm. T. Markham — an experienced civil engineer — for visiting the Battle-Ground, and preparing a map showing the movements of Captain Pausch during the Action of the 7th of October.

A word more concerning the Journal itself.

Pausch's Journal, the original MS. of which was recently found by Mr. Edward J. Lowell,

PREFACE

in the State Library at Cassel (Ständische Landesbibliothek) is among the most valuable of the Journals of the German Troops during the Revolution, that have yet been discovered — inasmuch as it gives with great fulness of detail, the difficulties which the Hessians experienced in going through the countries on the lower Rhine and Holland to the Seaboard. This manuscript, of one hundred and seventy pages, details the fate and fortune of Pausch and his men from May 15, 1776 (the day they left Hanau), to the close of Burgoyne's last battle, Oct. 7th, 1777. Hanau is on the Main. The vessels in which they there embarked, conveyed them to a transport at the mouth of the Waal, which took them to Spithead, to Quebec, and so to the river Sorel. The whole transit occupied three months and a half. To guard against desertion in passing through the free states on the Rhine, the vessels either anchored in the middle of the river, or were moored to islands. The transport had been engaged in the Guinea slave trade, and so was fit for the German slave trade. She started with one recalcitrant gunner in irons. The Journal also dwells freely on the personal experiences of its author and his men, while in Canada; and one thus gets glimpses into the private life of these execrated Hessian soldiers which make one lament their hard and unhonored fate. Both officers and men were cavalierly treated by their English comrades. English officers could command Germans; but German officers could have no authority over English soldiers; and an attempt was made to deprive Capt. Pausch's men of their side arms, when off duty.

The Journal, moreover, is most copious in describing the three battles in which Pausch and his battery took an active part, viz: the naval action against Arnold on Lake Champlain, and the battles on the 19th of September, and the 7th of October. In regard to the naval action, we are told by Pausch, that Arnold's heroism, and that of his men, made his conquerors afraid to move forward from Crown Point, or even to winter there. Pausch, who first met the rebels at Valcour, testifies to their firing so well as to sink one of his vessels, and firing still when their own were sinking. His minute account of this action, which tallies with Gen. Rogers' account in *Hadden's Journal,* must correct and complete those already in circulation. Regarding also the battles of Saratoga, Pausch's account is the first we have had of the part played by the *Hanau Artillery* in those actions, which well supplements that played at the same time by the Brunswick Infantry, as given in the *Military Journals of Gen. Riedesel.* In fact, no historian of these conflicts and no one interested in this portion of our Revolutionary history, can fail to learn something he would be glad to know, from the day book of this Hessian officer.

WILLIAM L. STONE.

Jersey City Heights, Dec. 1st, 1886.

INTRODUCTION.

THE town of Hanau lies upon the Main about a dozen miles above Frankfort, in the midst of a vast plain. The county of Hanau extended in the last century some forty-five or fifty miles east and west, but was in few places more than five miles wide. There were outlying pieces scattered here and there among the neighboring states, as was usual with German counties. Hither, in the year 1754, had come the Princess Mary, daughter of King George II, of England, and wife of Frederick, the Hereditary Prince of Hesse Cassel, who had lately avowed his conversion to the Catholic creed. "He was a brutal German," says Horace Walpole, "obstinate, of no genius, and after long treating the Princess Mary, who was the mildest and gentlest of her race, with great inhumanity, had for some time lived on no terms with her; his father, the Landgrave William protected her: an arbitrary, artful man, of no reputation for integrity."[1]

The Princess had been married fourteen years at the time of her separation from her husband, and she brought three sons with her to Hanau. The oldest, William, was independent Count of that territory. His cousin, King George III, was a surety for his independence, until the time should come for him to succeed his father at Cassel. William was a heartless pedant, fond of money and of pleasure. The business of letting out troops for hire was hereditary in his family, having been entered into by his great-grandfather, nearly a hundred years before, and pursued ever since that time. When, therefore, in the summer of 1775, the Hereditary Prince heard that his dear cousin was in difficulties in America, he wrote him the following letter.

---

[1] Memoirs of George II, Vol. I, p. 351.

[1]"THE HEREDITARY PRINCE OF HESSE CASSEL
TO KING GEORGE III.

Hanau, ce 19. août 1775.

Sire,

L'Epoque présente que les troubles suscités par les sujets de V. M^{té} dans une autre partie du monde ont fait naître, rallume le zéle et l'attachement de tous ceux qui pénetrés dé vos bontés, Sire, ne cessent de faire les voeux les plus ardens pour la felicité et le repos du meilleur des Rois.

Animé de ces sentiments que mon respect soumis et mon attachement inviolable pour sa Personne me dictent, je supplie V. M^{té} d'agréer favorablement que dans cet instant ou Elle paroit desirer des trouppes Allemandes j'ose lui offrir dans la moindre condition et à ses ordres mon Regiment d'Infanterie composé de cinq cent hommes, tous enfants du pays que la protection de V. M^{té} m'assure uniquement et tous prêts à sacrifier avec moi leur vie et leur sang pour son service.

Daignéz me pardonner la liberté que je prens et regarder l'intention et non la chose même.

---

[1] State Paper Office, Holland. Vol. 592, quoted in *Der Soldatenhandel deutscher Fursten nach Amerika von F. Kapp*, 1864.

Que ne puisse, je offrir 20 m. hommes à V. M^{té} ce seroit avec le même empressement. Qu'il lui plaise donc de disposer entièrement de mon Regiment à quel tems et où Elle ordonnera. Il est tout piêt au premier clin d'oeuil qu'Elle daignera m'en faire donner."

This letter was despatched under cover to Sir Joseph Yorke, the British ambassador at the Hague, who promptly transmitted it to London. On the 1st of September, the Earl of Suffolk, Secretary of State acknowledged the receipt of it to Sir Joseph.[1] "The nobleness of sentiment and affectionate attachment, which dictated His Serene Highness's offer, and the handsome manner in which it is expressed, cannot be sufficiently admired. His Majesty feels the extent of it all and will return an answer in his own hand."[2]

In the following November, Colonel William Faucitt received orders to negotiate with German princes, for troops to be used in America. His first bargains were made with the Duke of Brunswick and the Landgrave of Hesse Cassel,

---

[1] *Kapp, F. Der Soldatenhandel deutscher Fursten nach Amerika, p.* 227, 1864.

[2] State Paper Office, German States, Vol. 102, quoted in *Der Soldatenhandel deutscher Fursten nach Amerika von F. Kapp*, 1864.

the father of Prince William. On the 4th of February, 1776, the Colonel arrived at Hanau, and presented the following letter.

[1]King George III, to the Hereditary Prince of Hesse Cassel.

St. James, January 2, 1776.

Mon Cousin,

En consequence de ce que mon principal Secretaire d'Etat, le Comte de Suffolk, a eu l'honneur de vous écrire en mon nom, j'ai chargé le Col. Faucitt de se rendre à votre cour de vous présenter cette lettre de ma part et de réitérer les assurances de ma sensibilité, pour la maniére noble avec laquelle vous avez bien voulu m'offrir vos troupes. Je les accepte avec bien des remercimens et ayant muni le Col. Faucitt des pleni-pouvois nécessaires pour conclure une convention avec vous, je vous prie de donner créance entière à ce qu'il vous dira en mon nom, surtout quand il vous donnera des assurances de l'amitié et de l'estime, avec lesquelles je suis, *etc., etc.*"

The bargain was quickly concluded. On the

---
[1] Almon's Parliamentary register, Vol. 3, p. 300-302, 1776.

5th, Faucitt was able to send off to London, the following treaty.

"Be it known to all whom it may concern, that his Majesty the King of Great Britain having judged proper to accept a body of infantry of the troops of his most serene highness the hereditary Prince of Hesse Cassell, reigning Count of Hanau, &c., to be employed in the service of Great Britain, the high contracting parties have giving orders for this purpose to their respective ministers, that is to say, his Britannic Majesty to Colonel William Faucitt, captain of the guards; and the most serene hereditary Prince of Hesse Cassell to his minister and privy councillor Frederic de Malsbourg; who after the exchange of their respective full powers have agreed upon the following articles.

Art. I. The said Most Serene Prince yields to his Britannic Majesty a body of infantry of six hundred sixty-eight men, which shall be at the entire disposition of the King of Great Britain.

Art. II. The Most Serene Prince engages to equip compleatly this corps, and that it shall be ready to march the twentieth of the month of

March next, at farthest. The said corps shall pass in review before his Britannic Majesty's commissary at Hanau, if that can be done, or at some other place, as opportunity shall offer.

Art. III. The Most Serene Prince engages to furnish the recruits annually necessary; these recruits shall be delivered to his Britannic Majesty's commissary, disciplined and compleatly equipped: his Most Serene Highness will do his utmost that the whole may arrive at the place of their embarkation at the time his Majesty shall fix upon.

Art. IV. The service of his Britannic Majesty, and the preservation of the troops, requiring equally that the commanding officers and subalterns should be perfectly acquainted with the service, his Most Serene Highness will take proper care in the choice of them.

Art. V. The Most Serene Prince engages to put this corps on the best footing possible, and none shall be admitted into it but persons proper for campaign service, and acknowledged as such by his Britannic Majesty's commissary.

Art. VI. This corps shall be furnished with tents and all necessary equipage.

Art. VII. The King grants to this corps the ordinary and extraordinary pay, as well as all the advantages in forage, provisions, winter-quarters, and refreshments, &c., &c., enjoyed by the royal troops; and the Most Serene Prince engages to let this corps enjoy all the emoluments of pay that his Britannic Majesty allows them. The sick and wounded of the said corps shall be taken care of in the King's hospitals, and shall be treated in this respect as his Britannic Majesty's troops; and the wounded, not in a condition to serve, shall be transported into Europe, and sent back into their own country at the expence of the King.

Art. VIII. There shall be paid to his Most Serene Highness, under the title of levy money, for each foot soldier, thirty crowns *banco*; the crown reckoned at fifty-three sols of Holland: one half of this levy-money shall be paid six weeks after the signature of the treaty, and the other half, three months and a half after the signature.

Art. IX. According to custom, three wounded men shall be reckoned as one killed: a man killed, shall be paid for at the rate of the levy-money. If it shall happen that any company of this corps should be entirely ruined or destroyed, the King will pay the expence of the necessary recruits to re-establish this corps.

Art. X. The Most Serene Prince reserves to himself the nomination to the vacant employments, as also the administration of justice. Moreover his Britannic Majesty will cause orders to be given to the commander of the army in which this corps shall serve, not to exact of this corps any extraordinary services, or such as are beyond their proportion with the rest of the army; and when they shall serve with the English troops, or with other auxiliaries, the officers shall command (as the military service requires of itself) according to their military rank, and the seniority of their commissions, without making any distinction of what corps the troops may be with which they may serve. This corps shall take the oath of fidelity to his Britannic Majesty, without prejudice to that which they have taken to their sovereign.

Art. XI. Their pay shall commence fifteen days before the march of this body of troops, and from the time the troops shall have quitted their quarters, in order to repair to the place of their destination, all the expences of march and transport, as well as of the future return of the troops into their own country, shall be at the charge of his Britannic Majesty.

Art. XII. His Britannic Majesty will grant to the Most Serene Prince, during all the time that this body of troops shall be in the pay of his Majesty, an annual subsidy of twenty-five thousand and fifty crowns *banco*. His Majesty shall cause notice of the cessation of the aforesaid subsidy to be given, a whole year before it shall cease to be paid, provided that this notice shall not be given till after the return of the troops into the dominions of his Most Serene Highness.

This treaty shall be ratified by the high contracting parties, and the ratifications thereof shall be exchanged as soon as possible. In witness whereof, we the undersigned, in virtue of our

INTRODUCTION.

full powers have signed the present treaty, and have thereunto put the seals of our arms.

Done at Hanau, the 5th of February, 1776.

[L. S.] FREDERIC BN. DE MALSBOURG."
[L. S.] WILLIAM FAUCITT.

On the 17th of March, 1776, the Prince announced to King George the departure of his regiment in the following letter.

[1] THE HEREDITARY PRINCE OF HESSE-CASSEL TO KING GEORGE III.

Hanau, ce 17. Mars, 1776.

C'est avec ce respect et ce zèle sans bornes que les ordres de Votre Majesté m'inspirent à jamais, que je viens de faire partir avant-hier le 15. de ce mois mon régiment destiné à servir dans son armée. Le Colonel Faucitt m'ayant averti que le jour de départ devoit être accéleré autant que possible, je n'ai pas pérdu un instant pour cet effet. La liste ci-jointe que j'ose mettre devant Votre Majesté presentera l'état du régiment, comme j'en ai fait la revue Vendredi dernier,

---

[1] State Paper Office. German States, Vol. 103, quoted in *Der Soldatenhandel deutscher Fursten nach Amerika* ; von F. Kapp, 1864.

ainsi que les noms des officiers avec la date de leur patentes.

Puissiez-vous, Sire, avoir lieu d'être satisfait des faibles preuvses que j'ai desiré de vous donnez de mon devouement respectueux, de ma reconnaissance soumise. J'ose encore réiterer que mon ardeur inexprimable d'être utile a son service peut seule être nommée et non la chose même.

Permettez, Sire, que venant d'apprendre que le Landgrave, mon père, fournit à votre Majesté un Corps d'artillerie, j'ose lui offrir une compagnie de 120 hommes de cette espece appartenant jusqu'ici à mon régiment. J'en ai déjà fait la proposition au Colonel Faucitt, mais comme il n'avait pas d'ordre de prendre de l'artillerie en subsides, il n'a pas pu y entrer alors.

Des que j'apprendrai les intentions de Votre Majesté à cet égard cette compagnie pourra incessement marcher à ses ordres.

Cest avec, *etc., etc.*

The offer of the company of artillery abovementioned caused a long discussion. The prince wanted his subsidy increased, in proportion to the number of new men furnished. The Earl of Suffolk pointed out that His Serene Highness was already paid as highly per man as His Serene father. The prince, who, as we have seen, had hitherto conducted the correspondence in the diplomatic French of the period, now breaks into English.

[1] "THE HEREDITARY PRINCE OF HESSE-CASSEL TO THE EARL OF SUFFOLK.

Hanau, 1 May 1776.

My Lord!

The luck I have had to be able to show in some manner my utmost respect and gratitude to the best of Kings by offering my troops to His Majesty's service gives me a very agreeable opportunity of thanking you, My lord, for all your kindness and friendship to me upon that occasion and begging your pardon for all the trouble I may have provided you in this regard.

My only wishes are that all the officers and soldiers of my regiment, now to His Majesty's

---
[1] State Paper Office. German States, Vol. 104, quoted in *Der Soldatenhandel deutscher Fursten nach Amerika*; *von F. Kapp*. 1864.

orders, may be animated of the same respectful attachment and utmost zeal I shall ever bear for the king, my generous protector and magnanimous support. May the end they shall fight for answer to the kings upper contentment, and your laudable endeavors, My lord, be granted by the most happiest issue. The continuation of your friendship to me, Sir, which I desire very much assures your goodness and protection to my troops. I ask in their names this favor from you and hope they will deserve it.

"Excuse me, Sir, if I am not strong enough in the English language for to explain as I should the utmost consideration and sincere esteem with which I am for ever, My lord, your most humble and very obedient servant

"WILLIAM H. P. OF HESSE."

"THE EARL OF SUFFOLK
TO THE HEREDITARY PRINCE OF HESSE-CASSEL.

St. James, May 14, 1776.

Sir,

I am too deeply penetrated by the notice Your Serene Highness is pleased to take of me, not to beg your acceptance of my humble acknowledgments for your great condescension. The experience I have had of your Serene Highness sincere and affectionate attachment to the King has impressed indelible marks of gratitude and veneration on my breast. But proud as I shall be to show them upon all occasions, I am happy to assure your Serene Highness from a perfect knowledge of his Majesty's sentiments, that there is in this country a more powerful supporter of Your Serene Highnesses interests and a better advocate for any object you can recommend than any minister, be he ever so zealous, whom Your Serene Highness may honor with your commands.

Your troops, Sir, than which none can be finer or in a more complete condition, will certainly meet with every degree of protection and encouragement, and I make no doubt under the Blessing of God, share the high reputation of having preserved the lustre of that crown from which you are descended, the glory of that Monarch to whom in blood and principles you are so nearly allied, and the welfare of that nation of whose language your Highness has in so flattering and so accurate a manner shown your hereditary knowledge.

Permit me, Sir, to repeat the profound respect with which I have the honor, etc., etc."

"THE HEREDITARY PRINCE OF HESSE-HANAU TO THE EARL OF SUFFOLK.

Hanau, 21. July 1766.

Sir;

I can make no better use of your friendship and goodness to me than in recommending you, My lord, the propositions which my private Counsellor Malsburg directs in my name to you. My attachment and most humble respect to the best of kings removes all idea of interest in me. His Majesty's particular goodness assures me that he would [not] take ill, the desire I have to stay in a certain military relation with his service even after the present treaty's expiration.

I hope, My lord, you will find I do not ask too much, and in this regard I beg you to support this affair with your utmost credit. My gratitude will be without end, and shall only be compared to the greatest consideration—, I have the honor to be with for ever, My lord, your most humble and very obliged servant

WILLIAM H. P. OF HESSE."

The proposal, above referred to, which Counsellor Malsburg was to send, was nothing less than that the troops of Hesse-Hanau should remain in the English service for six years after the war. The request, of course, was extravagant. The Earl of Suffolk appears to have grown tired of bickering. In the latter part of 1776 he yielded to the solicitations of the Prince and the subsidy was increased by forty-five thousand crowns. Meanwhile the artillery had not been held back while the negotiations were pending. It left Hanau on the 15th of May, and its further adventures may best be traced in the journal of its commanding officer which is given in the following pages.

Little is known of Georg Pausch after Burgoyne's surrender. His signature appears on the Cambridge parole now in the Boston Public Library. In 1786 the County of Hesse-Hanau was united to the Landgraviate of Hesse Cassel through the death of Landgrave Frederick II, and the succession of his son William III. From that date we find the name of Georg Pausch entered in the official calendar of Cassel as major, in the regiment of light artillery. That regiment was quartered in the town of Cassel and in the fortresses of Ziegenhain, Hanau and Rheinfels. In which of these places Pausch had his quarters cannot be determined. His name disappears from the calendar in 1796, so that it is probable that he died early in that year or late in the year preceding. It is possible that a search in the archives of Marburg would bring to light more particulars about him. There are few events or persons connected with the Revolutionary war about which we might not hope for light from the same source.

The manuscript in the Ständische Landesbibliothek at Cassel was copied in 1868 from the original, which was then at Wilhelmshöhe, and is undoubtedly now at Marburg.

EDWARD J. LOWELL.

Pausch's Journal.

1776 May 15th, In conformity to the order of our Gracious Prince[1] the roll-call was beaten at half-past three P. M., and the company[2] marched out of the Mill-fortification to the Parade-ground, where all the necessary accoutrements for my men were found in readiness. A quarter of an hour afterwards, the signal was given by the tap of the drum for a forward movement; and, the lines being formed, we at once marched through the hospital Gate of the old town[3] to the wood-warehouses. Here the company immediately embarked on the ships, which had been designated for our transportation, in the presence of our most gracious sovereigns.

Our beloved Prince gave us a mark of his gracious and fatherly kindness by accompanying us for quite a long distance down the right

---

[1] Count William of Hesse-Hanau.
[2] It will be borne in mind that this is the Journal of the Company of the Hesse-Hanau artillery attached to the Hesse-Hanau Regiment. According to Eeelking, Pausch's Company consisted of 4 officers and 126 privates.
[3] Hanau.

bank of the river Main; an act which called forth the most loyal sentiments from the entire force which had been so graciously entrusted to my charge. At this point our journey began with many expressions of good will and wishes for our success on the part of those we were leaving: and here we saw for the last time in a long while our beloved Prince and Benefactor.[1] Here he bade us farewell; and we proceeded to Offenbach, where we anchored in the middle of the Main for the night.

16th. We left our moorings at 3 A. M., and passed Frankfort about 4:30. The sentinels and the different detachments of this garrison shouldered arms as we passed; but we were visited by no one, neither did we have to pass through any examination. At 11:30 we reached Mainz; and although I had sent ahead Lieut Spangenberg with the free-passes, we were obliged to land. Both ships were examined by two custom-house Inspectors. I immediately asked the reason of this; and in reply was told that it was done for the purpose, merely, of ascertaining whether the captain had not on board dutiable freight on his own account. As the Rhine was quite high, we sailed so rapidly that we reached Bingen about 6 o'clock the same evening. I then sailed

---

[1] How this "beloved Prince and Benefactor" must have "laughed in his sleeve" at these expressions from those whom, to get the means to gratify his passions, he was selling into slavery, and bartering like so many cattle!

toward Caub, and chose the island, where the so-called palace is situated, near which to drop anchor and rest for the night. I did this, because this spot was the best I could find for my men to take a little comfort by leaving the ships and sleeping on shore. I arrived here at 8 o'clock. The inhabitants of Caub were asked to bring some wine and other necessaries to my men and sell them for cash. This they promptly did.

17th. It chanced to be the weekly Market-Day at Caub; and I therefore delayed my departure until 7:30 o'clock in order to give my men an opportunity to lay in some provisions. For this purpose, (with the exception of the women) I sent ashore eighteen men, under the command of two officers and six subalterns; and in order that the purchases might be made without any disturbance, I myself, took a small boat half an hour in advance, and went to St. Goar. As I did not wish to be long absent from my men, and as I also desired to take advantage of the rise of the river[1] so as to make a quick passage, I was not able to call upon his Excellency, General von Wutgenau at the fortress of Rheinfels to announce that my company were passing down the Rhine. I however, made a statement to this effect to Maj. Gen. v. Marschalk (the commandant at St. Goar[2]) and requested him to

[1] Caused probably by the spring freshets.
[2] A town in the Prussian States on the west side of the Rhine, 16 miles south of Coblentz.

make my excuses to his Excellency, and to give him as a reason for my not waiting on him the responsibility devolving upon me on account of the near approach of my ships. The latter reached Rhinefels at 9 o'clock; and before they had come to the frontier of Cur-Trierische, (which lies nearly opposite St. Goar) I returned on board.

Since yesterday we have had a head wind; notwithstanding which, however, we passed Coblentz at one, Neuwied at four, Andernach at five, and Oberwinter at a quarter of nine where we anchored for the night.

P. N. Every morning I always order the *reveille* to be beaten at daybreak, and the tatoo in the evening.

The custom-house officers from Hanau, have exercised the greatest politeness towards those officers and subalterns who were sent in advance.

So far, pleasure, contentment, and excellent health prevail among my men. They never fail, after *reveille* and tatoo, to make their offerings due their God by singing morning and evening hymns for one hour. Afterwards, they give themselves up to enjoyment, but in such a manner as never to give me cause for complaint or punishment. I cannot sufficiently praise the good feeling shown by my three officers while on duty; nor can I adequately express my satisfaction especially at the trouble they take to maintain good order and acquire the confidence of my men. I must confess that all my men have already acquired more confidence than I had anticipated at Hanau. I have therefore pardoned the cannonier, Bischle, who had been placed under arrest, and released him from his chains.

Continuation.

May 18th. During the night of the 17th and 18th, we rested quietly near Ober Winter; and in the morning precisely at 4 o'clock, we left our moorings, passing Bonn at 6 o'clock, and reaching the Imperial city of Cöln at 10 o'clock. I anchored about a thousand yards[1] above the town. From here I despatched two officers (Spangenberg and Bach), the sergeant and nine subalterns, and a few men from each detachment to Cöln (with six loaded and as many unloaded guns) for the purpose of having their money, which they had brought from Erfurt, exchanged for local currency. They were also directed to buy provisions. As this is a large place, I was obliged to anchor and wait a long while for their return. We were all re-united about 2 o'clock P. M. when we at once proceeded still farther on our way as far as Zons[2]

---

[1] Or literally a thousand paces.
[2] A town on the Rhine having an historic castle; 13 miles N. N. West of Cologne, and 50 N. E. of Liege.

Had it not been that both yesterday afternoon and to-day the wind was ahead, we should now be still farther on our journey. It was half past eight by the time we reached Zons, and we accordingly remained here overnight. As the water of the Rhine was very rough on account of a heavy gale during the day, we were forced to anchor till the next morning.

19th. We were compelled to wait till 7 o'clock A. M., before sailing, by which time the Rhine had become calmer. At one o'clock, we passed Düsseldorf; and at five o'clock reached Buckroth. This is the first station of the Prussian Custom-House, and I had accordingly sent on here in advance Lieut. Spangenberg with the Royal free-pass. As soon as we came opposite the town, the Custom-House officers, accompanied by my Lieutenant, rowed out towards us. They did not subject us to any examination, but contented themselves with rowing around my ship and wishing us a pleasant journey. They, however, made an indorsement on the back of the Royal pass to the effect that we passed the station at such an hour. I nevertheless thought it best when we arrived at the next Custom Station, to send a note ashore to the officials stating that we had passed the upper station free by virtue of the Royal free-pass. In the evening we anchored an hour's sail above N. Wesel, and remained there during the night.

20th. At 6 in the morning I took a boat and went ahead to the town, where I showed the pass to his Excellency Lt. Gen. and Commander Von Solomons. I also exhibited particularly to him the Prince's order relating to the refunding of 42 ducats at Emmerich. In reply, his Excellency said that this had most likely been already attended to; but that if it had not, it would now be fixed. At the same time he assured me that if he could aid us in any way whatever, he would do so with pleasure. This he did to show his great regard and friendship for us. My ships arrived about two hours afterwards; and I immediately got under way for Emmerich. There I showed my free-passes, at the same time calling the attention of the custom officers to the refunding of the money which had been taken from the Hanau Regiment. They assured me that this had already been done in accordance with the gracious order of the Prussian Major. I then asked them to give me a paper certifying both that this had been done and where, that I might send the same to the Prince.[1] My request was at once complied with; and this document I have filed under Letter A. I intended to have made good headway this evening, but a gale, beginning to blow, drove us close into shore about two hour's sail above Schenken-Schanz,

---

[1] Prince William of Hanau.

where, finding a quiet spot, we rested for the night.

21st. As soon as the *reveille* was beaten I ordered an advance, and shortly reached Schenken-Schanz, to which place I had already sent on ahead, Lieut. Spangenburg and the boatman, Becktell with the Government pass. This was the first Dutch Revenue station, and our ships were forbidden to go farther. The officials told us that they had received no instructions to pass us. They further said, that as we could not produce a Dutch free pass signed by our Prince every thing would have to be appraised and the duty paid. But as I did not feel like complying, and, moreover, was unable [from lack of money] to do it, even had I been so disposed, I returned at full speed to Arnheim where the Revenue officers of the Admiral were supposed to be stationed. I sought there in vain for such information as would enable our expedition to proceed; and even asked the assistance of his Excellency Von Nieuenheim, commander of the Baden Infantry stationed there. This latter personage took an interest in the matter, and reported it to the City President. But even this step was of no avail. Whoever I questioned gave me the same answer, viz: that his Highness must first give his permission. It was 11 o'clock when I arrived at Arnheim from Schenken Schanz; and until two o'clock I lingered among these ill-bred people, when, finally, even the officers of their own garrison became angry with them. Thus circumstanced I made up my mind quickly, and took an express-post to the Hague. I left Arnheim at 2 P. M., travelled the entire night, and arrived at the house of his Excellency's Ambassador, Sir Yorke Logie, in Hague at 6 A. M., having come by way of Utrecht and Leyden.

22d. I immediately awoke his Secretary who announced my arrival to his chief. To him I reported the trouble I had met with, which had made the progress of our march difficult. The Knight lost no time in going to the Court at 8 A. M. and laying the matter before his Highness, the Governor of the States. Thereupon, my free passes were promised me by 10 the same morning. Time passed. It was 10, 11, 12, then 1 o'clock in the afternoon! I then received an invitation to dine with his Excellency the Knight, Sir Yorke Logie; and at the close of the dinner, or about 6 P. M., I received my papers, and also a large package addressed to Col. Rainsford at Nimwegen, who had left the Hague for this place a day in advance in order to inspect my company.

23d. I took the same route back, viz: by way of Leyden and Utrecht; then bore to the left to Nimwegen, where I arrived on the 23d at half past eleven in the morning. Here I received a document giving us a free passage *not* from Schenken Schanz down the Rhine to Arnheim, but on the Wahl to Nimwegen! Moreover, as soon as I should arrive there I would have to pass another inspection, and this notwithstanding my assertion that all had been seen to, and provided for, by his Excellency, the English Col. Faucit at Hanau! And now I was given to understand that the whole routine would have to be again gone through with in conformity to the special order of his Excellency, the Ambassador, which Col. von Rainsford showed me. Accordingly, I hastened to leave Nimwegen that I might rejoin my men at 3 P. M. the same day. The rest of the day was spent by the soldiers in cleaning and painting the ships, and by the officers, subalterns and myself in preparing different rolls, which will be found under Letters B. C. and D.

24th. My orders were to leave Schanken Schanz at day-break, but the wind prevented me from doing so; and although I sailed some miles I was obliged to return to the shore. On this account, we only reached Nimwegen, opposite the parade-ground, at a quarter past five. Accompanied by Col. Dufais, I started an hour in advance to announce the arrival of the artillery to Col. Rainsford. In the Wahl, where we came to anchor, there is a small island. Here I had the men land and formed in companies.

The above mentioned Col. Rainsford, accompanied by his Highness, Prince of Waldeck's Colonel and Commander Von der Hooven, and the greater part of the staff-officers of the garrison, paid me a visit while at this spot. As they left the boats and passed along our front, I ordered the march to be beaten and the men to give the usual salute. I then gave the command, "Turn right;" on which the officers and subalterns advanced to the centre of the company and reformed the front.

The colonel was present at roll-call and mustered the men himself; looked over each soldier critically; and expressed his satisfaction at the general appearance of all the men. Finally, I formed the company into four sections and caused them to salute while passing. I then asked for further instructions, and was told that the men must take the oath of fealty to their Majesties.[1] My reply was, that if desired, I would order my men to pass before them for review twice more, but that it would be useless to oblige them to take the oath again, as that formality had been properly attended to at Hanau in the presence of the English Col. Faucit; and further, by that oath, each one of my men was bound to be faithful and loyal towards the King. As no objection was made to this remark, I ordered the men to sheathe their bayonets, file to

[1] King George III and Prince William of Hanau.

the left, and return in single file into the ship. This second parade took up one hour.

This entirely unexpected delay gave rise to several annoyances. 1st It caused an expenditure of 121 Dutch florins for the post-chaise and drink-money, for the living and drink of the Post riders, and for horses and road and custom-house fees. All this was incurred by the journey from Schenken Schanz[1] to Arnheim and the Hague[2], back to Nimwegen, and from Nimwegen to Schenkan Schanz: 2d On account of this three days' delay my men were short of their rations for just that length of time; and 3d, the sailing-master Bechtel was out of pocket 76 to 78 florins by this delay which caused extra expenses for the wheel-man, himself and his sailors. All this I reported to the Ambassador at the Hague, stating, at the same time, that as this had all happened without any fault on our part, these expenses should properly be charged to the King's account. That personage immediately approved of it thinking the amount reasonable; and I handed to Colonel Rainsford the necessary orders for the repayment. Accordingly, my travelling expenses of 121 florins were

---

[1] A strong fortress of Guilderland, situated in an angle of the Betuwe where the Rhine divides into two branches. It occupies a commanding position and is considered as the centre of communication between Germany and Holland.

[2] A large and beautiful town in the Netherlands. As long ago as 1250 it became the residence of the Governors or Counts of Holland; and since that period, it has been, almost without interruption the seat of government. It is especially celebrated for its porcelain manufactures.

handed to me, as soon as the review was over, the same day. The provisions, also, which had been ordered the previous day by **Col.** von der Hooven by order of Col. von **Rainsford**, were delivered immediately after the drill. The bill of the sailing-master, which I had already approved was countersigned by Col. Rainsford, but not paid, as this item belonged to the contract made by Col. Faucit at Hanau. It would be perfectly inexcusable should this man receive nothing for his losses. He took good care of the transportation, and was ever ready to give friendly aid even to the most inconsiderable man in the company; so that he possesses the love and confidence of every common soldier. We all desired if it were a possible thing, that he should bring us as far as Quebec.

With all the above mentioned matters the 24th passed; and we spent the night on the Island off which we anchored.

25th. The company were obliged to start at day-break. By order of the Colonel, I left the command with Lieutenant Spangenberg, who, with Lieut. Bach remained with the men; and in company with the Colonel and Lieut. Dufais set out from Nimwegen[1] in a small yacht for

---

[1] Famous from the Congress held there under the mediation of Charles II; and for the peace concluded at and ratified by William the III in 1678. Situated on the left bank of the great branch of the Rhine called the Waal. It is fortified with walls and ditches and extensive out works. Taken by the French, 8th Sept., 1794.

Dortrecht[1] at 11 o'clock that same morning. Our object was to look for our transport-ship; and this we found, on the afternoon of the 26th, on the "Kiel," a great canal about a short mile distant from Wilhelmstadten.[2] The Colonel and ourselves boarded it that we might personally inspect the ship, and also make arrangements with the Captain for the boarding and accommodation of our men. The presence of the Colonel and of Lieut. Dufais was very necessary in perfecting these arrangements, as the Captain spoke only English except a very little French; indeed, he spoke even less French than myself. Our ship, which is called the "Juno" is a three-master, and is commanded by Captain Edward Schmidt, a very quiet and pleasant Englishman of, perhaps, 38 years of age. The "Juno" is not a common transport-ship. It presents a neat appearance, and was formerly engaged in the Slave-trade. She carries on her front decks 18 short iron ship cannon; but, at present, has on board only seven pieces of 4 and 6 lbs calibre. The captain intends to make up his full complement of cannon at Portsmouth. The Colonel informed me that

---

[1] Dortrecht or Dort, a town in the Netherlands in S. Holland. It suffered in 1421, by a terrible inundation which breaking down the dykes swept away 72 villages and drowned 100,000 people. The timber which is brought in immense floats down the Rhine is here prepared for use in the saw-mills and exported. The place is also famous from the famous synod of Dort having been held here in 1618 and 19, an assembly of Protestant divines which condemned the tenets of the Armenians.

[2] A strongly fortified town in Holland, on that part of the Meuse called Buttervliet. It is one of the Keys of Holland, and defended with 7 bastions and double fosse. It has also an excellent harbor

in case of an emergency, my men would be expected to help serve the cannon; and that, if the ship should be attacked, we must all turn to and aid in defending it to our utmost ability. This request, together with the English order, I kept to myself, only communicating them to Lieut. Dufais and the other officers; for I resolved only to tell my men of what was expected of them when the emergency should arise, hoping, by this course, to keep them from becoming timid, and perhaps, as it might prove, without reason.

The bedsteads and the small mattrasses and quilts are of middling quality, good or bad as you have a mind to call them. I, therefore, gave them the company's covers. It was difficult to find accommodations for the company on this ship. The beds, six in number, are very narrow and are arranged in two tiers one above the other, and separated. Every six men receive their provisions together. To every Corporal's squad, I give one officer and eleven common soldiers. The married men and women occupy the beds; and to prevent misbehaviour as much as possible, every three pairs are separated.[1] My three officers and myself have a pretty large cabin, the wainscotting, upholstering and table of which are very neatly finished in Mahogany. After spending about an hour and a half in our inspection and in completing our final arrange-

---

i. e. Three pairs to each bed.

ments, we started back to Dortrecht. We had, on the 25th, scarcely left Nimwegen at 11 o'clock, when we found that our Hanau ships with the artillery had been again arrested, and we were once more obliged to pay revenue duties. By the merest luck, the English Colonel, who was with us, had Holland money. For a permit to proceed he had to pay 33 florins, and for the passage-money of the Hanau Regiment, 12 florins and 16 stuber. Nor until these sums had been actually paid down in our presence, were we allowed to proceed on our voyage. Indeed, these Holland formalities were of such a nature that had not the Colonel chanced to be present with the money, a second journey to the Hague would have been unavoidable.

On the 25th two craft, called lighters, were chartered at Dortrecht and sent back to meet the Hanau ships a little distance from Herrtenfelds where they were reloading.

26th. In this lighter, containing one-half of the men, the six cannon, one gun-carriage, one cart, and the greater part of the baggage, I started ahead from Dortrecht, at half past one, for the transport ship, arriving there at about a quarter past three. I immediately set about transferring the contents of the small vessel to the large one; but I had not yet finished my work when, three hours later, the other lighter arrived with the rest of the men and the buggy, and also with the Colonel and Lieutenant Dufais. Every thing was then, in the wink of an eye, transferred from the lighters to the transport vessel the same night.

Notwithstanding all this, the vessel chosen for the purpose is altogether too small. The following two days were spent in arranging matters and putting things to rights. The cannons, together with the gun-carriages, were lowered into the hold of the ship on top of the ballast and barrels, but in such a way that many repairs will be necessary when we take them up again on account of the smallness of the space. Every thing else is still between decks. (N. B. as no place could be found for the large casks containing the harnesses for the horses, they had to be all unpacked, and after being folded up and tied together they were taken to the hold of the vessel, together with the ropes, bags, mangers, and pouch-bags.) The Captain will have to, and indeed, intends, to procure an additional and smaller vessel either at Portsmouth or Spithead, so that the space between decks may be clear, free, and open.

27th. We sailed from the place where we embarked, Colonel Rainsford taking leave of us and starting for the Hague. Before he took his departure, he sent to London by the Packet-boat from Helvoetsluys[1] a large package addressed to His Majesty, the King of Great Britain. We passed Wilhelmstadt within a quarter of a mile of Helvoetsluys, where we cast anchor, and here in this road we are now.

28th.
29th.
30th.
31st. We are still here, in consequence of contrary winds; but as soon as the wind changes, we will not hesitate, if the change is favorable, to get under sail for our place of destination and rendezvous.

Up to the present time, we are all well and healthy having escaped catching the itch of Bombadier Wall, S. C., who has it terribly. I have him sleep all alone. Unfortunately, the surgeon on board has no remedy for this disease with him, nor can he procure any until we arrive at Portsmouth. Since the 27th, every body has to take up with the ship's table. We all find the food pretty palatable as yet. The beer is passable and drinkable, It is called "small beer" in English.

The men, moreover, among themselves are cheerful and contented.

---

[1] A fortified town in S. Holland having a very large and an excellent harbor; also extensive magazines, dock-yards and a naval school; at this time and for a long while after, it was the regular station for packets to England.

Colonel Rainsford thoroughly understands our profession, and has been entirely favorable to us. Accordingly, Dufais and myself, while with him in his yacht, had to undergo a systematic and extended examination; at the result of which he appeared very much pleased. We drew plans and manœuvred while in our little yacht, but, of course, only on paper! He enquired minutely into my administration of the Company, as to the amount of clothing on hand, etc.; and upon my specifying every thing I had on hand, and also telling him what I had given to each new man, he expressed his entire satisfaction. He was, also, particularly gratified on being told that each company, by order of his most serene Highness the Prince, were supplied with an equally good outfit and, in some instances, perhaps a better.

He took notes of all these details, and assured me that he would make a favorable report both to his Majesty, the King, and to the Ambassador.

The troops of the Duke of Brunswick, on the contrary, were poorly provided with these necessary articles, having very little, if indeed, anything with them.

Second Continuation of the Journal, which ended May 31st.

1776, June 1st. We rode at anchor in the roadstead of Helvoetsluys until the following morning. At half past eight, the anchors were weighed, and we made sail with a favorable, though high wind. This favorable wind lasted no longer than till evening when it veered round and became unfavorable. However, we continued on our course until morning.

2d. No wind whatever; and we could scarcely notice that we were moving. By 12 o'clock at noon the wind became again favorable, but was still very weak. Towards 3 o'clock it became stronger again, but being rather ahead delayed our progress.

3d. However, we continued on, and reached the Channel about 9 o'clock on the morning of June 3d, with a favorable but scarcely a noticeable breeze. Towards 6 o'clock in the evening, a thunder-shower gathered, but it passed off towards the French coast. Towards half past eight in the evening, another terrible thunder storm arose accompanied by terrific lightning and a very severe wind; which latter, although at first favorable for us, soon afterward became contrary. This weather lasted until midnight. The Captain felt considerable alarm, for we were pretty close to two sand-banks in the channel; and the worst of all was, that it was night.

4th. After midnight, the danger seemed to vanish; by two in the morning the wind was favorable; by nine and ten it was still favorable but high; and at half past ten we reached the roadstead of Spithead where we cast anchor.

Continuation of the Interrupted Journal at Spithead.

June 4th. After mailing my letters and humble reports, I enquired at what time, the remainder of the Hessian and Brunswick troops, and, also, those of Waldeck, were expected to arrive; but at this time I could learn nothing definite about them. Thus passed the 5th, 6th, 7th, 8th, 9th, 10th and 11th.

12th. The three transports, with troops of the Duke of Brunswick, arrived today under the command of Col. von Specht, one of the transport-ships containing his own regiment.

14th. Having known Col. von Specht during the last war,[1] I called on him and enquired after the rest of the troops, but he knew nothing about them. Regarding himself, however, he said, that in consequence of continuous contrary winds his ship was thirteen days in coming from the neighborhood of Stade;[2] in fact, that the vessel had not done much more than drift; and

---

[1] The "Seven Years War."
[2] A town in the Dutchy of Bremen on a small river about a mile from the Elbe; formerly the capital of a country and the residence of the Counts. It possesses a strong fort. General Riedesel passed through this place on his way to Canada.

that he had had to put up with many disagreeable things. The Brunswick troops, he said, had all sailed at the same time; and that those of the ships which were still missing had been driven out of their course by the wind, and had thus become separated from the others. He had also heard that at the time he started, some Hessian troops had embarked in only two vessels; and it was said that seven transports were still required for the rest.

15th. After the 15th had passed, the missing ships, containing the Brunswick troops, arrived on the 16th in the offing; also the Waldeck Regiment.

16th. Some of the vessels entered the harbor of Spithead the same evening; and some early the following morning.

17th. Of the last comers, I have seen none as yet. Lieuts. Spangenberg and Bach went to-day to Portsmouth on a furlough. On their return, they reported that the Hessian troops would arrive without fail on the 21st or 22d of this month. But before that time arrived, a captain of a vessel brought the news, that the Brunswick and Waldeck troops, the Scheiter recruits, the horses destined for the Burgoyne Light Dragoon Regiment, and the artillery and baggage, under the escort of two frigates, would sail [direct] for Quebec. How much truth there is in these reports, will be seen between now and to-morrow.

All the transports, now in this roadstead, are being supplied with water and provisions for a quarter of a year; and, in order that there may be room on board for the men and ourselves, my six cannon, gun carriages, boxes, chests, two carts, one wagon, blacksmith's tools, horses, harnesses, ropes, tent-poles and other necessaries were put on board a smaller vessel of two masts, called the "Gloucester." All my men, for the purpose of keeping good order in future, I keep together on my transport, "Juno." It was intended that I should send on board the "Gloucester," which carries our "traps," twenty-four men; but I refused to do so, on the ground that there was ample room on the "Juno" for all.

On one of the Brunswick transport-ships where I had visited Col. von Specht (a large Holland vessel called the "Freesland"), there were 450 men not counting the women and children. Even after occupying the deck three times, alternately, they cannot inhale the fresh air. The Colonel, himself, with sixteen officers and the Ship-Captain, all occupy a cabin not much larger than ours. For the privates, there are three tiers of bunks one on top of the other. There will be a great deal of sickness among these poor people on account of their great number, and the small space allotted to them. It is said, too, that there is another vessel containing 550 men, nearly an entire battalion. Col. Specht at once despatched a Captain to London, to call the attention of his Majesty the King, himself, to this state of affairs and beg him to change it.

19th. The day passed without the arrival of more vessels.

20th. About 3 o'clock in the afternoon, a whole fleet of Holland transports hove in sight; and as they came nearer under a good breeze we were pretty certain that they contained Hessian troops, a surmise which proved correct when, about 6 o'clock in the evening, they cast anchor in the road. Some of these ships sailed closer in towards Portsmouth[1] near the harbor; and it is reported that they had on board coal and other goods

The two Regiments of Wultginau and Bunan were recognized this evening; but the others are as yet unknown to me, as they are still a good

---

[1] Speaking of Portsmouth as it was at this time, Mrs. Reidesel says:

"Portsmouth is an agreeable seaport, and that which makes it the more interesting as a residence is, that one has a fine view of the ships which arrive daily, and announce themselves by firing cannon. Then the people run down to the shore, and with great impatience await their arrival in port. Ships are built here, and the dockyard is splendid, as is, also, the building in which those young men, who are intended for the marine service, are educated. Never have I before seen such order and cleanliness in a public school. Since my visit it has been entirely destroyed by fire. The house of the admiral is beautiful, and the view from it magnificent. A wall encircles the city, affording handsome walks. There are also, many beautiful houses in Portsmouth, and the people, though mostly sailors, are more civil than in Bristol. The admiral took care that they should be so, and punished all irregularities with severity, but in other respects he was a good and kind man."

distance off. After bed-time some more of these vessels came in sight; and the probability is, that with the splendid good wind, now prevailing, they will certainly arrive in time and will anchor here.

Continuation of Diary from Spithead near Portsmouth.

21st. 22d. During the night of the 21st and 22d all the Hessian troops of the Third Division dropped in one by one in Holland Transports and anchored in the road-stead To these troops, the Prince of Waldeck's Battalion, it is said, will be added. Our transport was, by this time, supplied with all the necessary provisions and ready to sail. With the greatest impatience we waited from hour to hour for the order to start. I went once more and for the last time, to Portsmouth both to learn something definite and to buy some provisions for myself. Here I met, the same morning, many Hessian officers and acquaintances, and among them Stude, the Envoy of Hesse-Cassel, Capt. von Kurtzleben of the Infantry Regiment, and von Donop[1] who was

---

[1] Count von Donop, the brave Hessian colonel, who fell at the Battle of Red-Bank, N. J., Oct. 22d, 1777, aged 37 He was found by the French officer, Capt. Duplesse, lying helpless on the battle-field among the dead and wounded, and brought to the house of a Quaker, where he lay three days in agony before he expired. Almost his last words to Duplesse, who had tenderly nursed him, were: "I die in the arms of honor, a sudden termination for a glorious career; but I die the victim of my ambition, and of the avarice of my prince!"

at the same hotel where I stopped, and whom I accordingly visited at his room, as I had ascertained he was then alone. I was received in a very friendly and hearty manner by this statesman and courtier; and after being entertained by him for nearly a quarter of an hour, I called upon our bankers, Taylor and Guitton, for the purpose of hearing the news and of bidding them farewell; for I knew now, to a certainty, through the English Quarter-Master General of our fleet (an officer of the Marines), that we would surely sail in a few days with the Brunswick troops for Quebec under sealed orders.

While waiting at the Bankers, I met an army pay-master, one Schmidt of the third division of the Hessian army. He was obliged to exchange his 40,000 Thalers for small bank-notes of five pounds sterling each, instead of guineas. This went sadly against the grain; and I saw clearly that he would very naturally have preferred good hard guineas. The same offer was also made to me, viz: that I should take as many small notes as I was in need of. I expressed my thanks but did not avail myself of their offer, saying that I had as many of them as I should need before arriving at Quebec, as my men were now all on board the ship; and, consequently, would not require any money. I also said, that I hoped, after arriving there[1], that I should receive genuine

---

[1] *i. e.* Quebec.

money, not those little bits of paper[1]; and farther, that I intended to pay my men for their services in real money till we arrived [in America]. My chief reason, however, — and it was not inconsistent with the above excuse — was this; that in case of an accident to the ship or to us, the little quantity of money we had on board might be more easily saved. I had intended, after finishing all my business, to go on board the vessel at about 7 o'clock, but the weather was so stormy, that no one would risk his life by going out to the ship in a small boat; and his life would really have been greatly endangered. I attempted it twice between 8 and 9 o'clock but each time was driven back to the shore.

22d. Finally, after many dangers, I started in my boat the next morning between 8 and 11 o'clock, on the 22d; but I was obliged to get on board a ship anchored quite a distance from mine, and on which were the Hessian Chasseurs and Grenadiers, and there wait until the fury of the storm had abated and my clothes had dried. This was not until afternoon.

Every thing was sinfully extravagant and dear, during the whole time of our stay, both for officers and privates. This remark applies to every necessary article for our use. All imaginable provisions were daily brought by vendors from the city in small boats to each ship for

[1] Had Pausch lived in our day he "Bland Silver dollar!" would probably have gone in for the

sale; but bread and every thing else was so dear that the men could hardly afford to buy them. Otherwise, Portsmouth and its surroundings are very pleasant.

The city itself, judging from outward appearance, consists of well built houses, although there are many small dwellings in the side streets and suburbs. To the west of it, is a large and extensive building with big gardens attached. This is the Hospital for all the sick soldiers and sailors of the King. Others, however, may become inmates by obtaining permission. To the east is the citadel, which, as well as the city near the road stead, is fortified by many large iron cannons. On the landside, also, the place is enclosed by the most durable works. The harbor, the wharfs — in fact, the shops for the building and repairing of ships, the anchor works and other blacksmith-shops, the depôt for provisions and the arsenals are all well worthy of inspection. Especially noteworthy is the astonishing number of iron ship-cannon — of from 48 to 12 and 6 pounders — with the large quantity of balls, and the awfully big anchors. But the handsomest appearance of all was made by the Manual transport frigate, which was anchored in the road. Many other ships were also gathered here in considerable numbers. The place, itself, which is not extensive, deserves, on account of the above objects of curiosity, to be visited in preference to many other towns. It should be seen particularly during the working hours of the ship-builders. A visitor, also, should glance at the front of the Arsenal where are situated the cannon, mortars, and the balls.

23d and 24th. During the 23d and 24th the Brunswick troops were supplied with their provisions. The provisioning of the Hessian soldiers was also begun. On the evening of the 24th, the above mentioned officer of Marines, viz: the former Quarter-Master General, inspected the number of our Marines. He also looked over the list of the Captain commanding the ship on which was my company. He then told us that we would sail on the morrow, and hoped and wished that we would reach our destination after a pleasant voyage.

25th. A little past 3 o'clock in the afternoon, our anchors were hoisted, and, under the protection of the two frigates, "Amazon" and "Garland," we sailed with the rest of the transports as far as the Island of St. Helena[1] where we all again cast anchor. This Island is from six to seven miles distant from Portsmouth, and, as my ship's Patron[2] describes it, 15 English miles long and about the same in width. It is inhabited; and is very pleasant and fertile. Here I counted our fleet, which was separated

---

[1] Pausch (probably from lack of knowledge of English) was misled, and confused the Bay of *St. Helens* in the Isle of Wight, with the Island itself. He means the Isle of Wight.

[2] *i. e.* The Captain.

from the rest at Spithead. It consists, including our ship, of 30 transports, and the above mentioned frigates, of which the "Amazon" leads the van, and the "Garland" brings up the rear. The entire fleet, therefore, consists of 32 ships. One of these ships carries our company with all of its "traps" and accoutrements; while eighteen others have on board the troops of the Duke of Brunswick, Scheiter's recruits, the horses for the Light Dragoon Regiment of Burgoyne, and the artillery and baggage.

The commander of the fleet — so far as relates to the ships themselves — is Capt. Jacobs, a Swede by birth; but the Brunswick troops are under the command of Col. von Specht.

26th. At a quarter past four in the afternoon, the signal shot was fired; the sails, hitherto lowered, were hoisted; the anchors were weighed; and, without further delay and with a fine east wind, we sailed; and thus, at last, we had made a good start upon our journey.

27th. During this day we kept generally alongside of the fleet, ours being the ship nearest the frigate which led the advance. But as the dusk of evening came on, the commander of the "Amazon" saw that our Captain, although only under half sail, had to hold back his ship with all his might, since, of all the other transports, it cut its way the quickest through the waves;

in fact, sailing as well as the fastest frigate. The "Amazon's" Commander, accordingly ordered our captain to lower those sails which were still unfurled, and to sail in front of his frigate, directing him at the same time, however, not to lose sight of the fleet. The Captain did as ordered and placed our ship in the van. But, as in consequence of the night, all the ships were obliged to separate somewhat from the rest in order to avoid an untoward collision, and as, furthermore, the darknesss rendered it impossible to keep the fleet in view, we found, at day-break of the 28th, that we had entirely separated from it. We could not, indeed, see a single vessel. We were now alone on the open sea without the company of our transports and the protection of our frigates; and the 29th and 30th past in a fruitless attempt to rejoin them.[1]

At the end of these two days we gave up all hope of again meeting them : the wind was unfavorable : we could make but little progress : we could only tack.

July 1st. No wind: indeed, far less than on the previous two days. In twenty-nine hours, we made scarcely as many English miles. The same evening, however, a breeze sprang up of such a nature as to cause the sea to become very

---

[1] Corroborated by Riedesel, who writes, "The transports had left England simultaneously with the vessel having on board the Hesse-Hanau artillery ; but the latter, soon becoming separated from the rest of the convoy, got the lead."

boisterous. After twenty-four hours, however, the angry waves quieted down, but the head wind still continued, so that little headway was made in a westerly direction.

4th, 5th and 6th. The wind seemed gradually to become more and more auspicious — though not all that could be desired — until the morning of the 7th, when, at a quarter past seven, the wind became perfectly favorable and the sea calm and propitious for our progress. On the evening of the same day, about a quarter of 7, we perceived approaching us a small two-master. Our Captain recognized it as an American privateer or pirate. He therefore ordered his six cannon to be got in readiness for action, and also the small arms for the sailors, which consisted of guns, pistols, blunderbusses, and long terrible Israelitish cimeters[1]. My men, also, who were not yet sea-sick were made ready for the emergency. The subalterns and my best cannoniers I armed with the twelve muskets which I had. I could not help feeling sorrowful at the lack of muskets, for, otherwise, I might have armed my entire company.

8th. Towards morning, about a quarter past one, the American Corsair was within gun-shot. We saluted it by three sharp cannon shot, following each other in slow succession, as a sign

---

[1] Pausch calls them "Israelitish," but he probably meant *Damascus* cimeters. The knowledge of the East at this time was not exhaustive; and anything from Syria or the East had, in his mind, a Jewish cast!

for it to halt. Whereupon, it hung out from the mast-head a lighted lantern, furled its sails and waited. Upon hailing it through a speaking-trumpet, the captain ascertained that it was only a French fishing smack, bound for the great fishing banks of Newfoundland, which France, under certain conditions, holds in common with England. These banks are situated between Cape Race[1] and St. Peter's Bank, 150 English miles in front of the above mentioned Cape almost in mid-ocean. The captain went in one of our boats on board the vessel and found that the master of the smack had stated things correctly.

For six days this fishing smack had sailed under favorable winds — the same winds which to us had been so inauspicious. The fact that it was night, had, it seems, caused our ship to be taken for the English frigate "Juno," and to be respected accordingly. This was quite an innocent honor! Another vessel of the same kind appeared a few hours later; and, again, it was taken, in the distance, to be an American privateer. We went through the same manœuvres as before, and with the same result; as it turned out, as above hinted, to be another French fishing smack. The French Captain requested our Captain, upon landing, to insert in a Newspaper, that the English transport "Juno," having on

[1] Pausch refers of course, to Cape Ray, opposite Cape Breton.

board the Hanau Artillery, had met his vessel on her way to America. Regarding our ship having been mistaken for the "Juno" by the first vessel, Capt. Schmidt of our ship gave that out for a fact; and it was no doubt so reported in some of the newspapers.

During these defensive preparations, and while it was yet supposed that the vessels were privateers, there was considerable downheartedness among both the young and old — particularly when the cannon were firing. However, after a little while all hands, except those who were sea-sick, came up, with sabres in their hands, ready for fighting. The sabres, however, were so short that they would have been of no use for blood-letting unless the enemy had boarded the ship. I was in the greatest dilemma on account of the paucity of muskets; for with those 18[1] we might have been captured.

12th. Our ship continued on without any more of such obstacles. The wind, however, continued more adverse than favorable, constantly driving our vessel in a zig-zag course, now to the right, and now to the left, whereby we made but little progress. Towards a quarter of nine the wind began to get astonishingly strong. The waves roared around the ship to the height of two-thirds of the main-mast. This

[1] 12? See *Ante*.

caused considerable commotion in the ship, so that no one could stand, much less walk, and this lasted fully twenty-four hours.

13th. Towards 9 o'clock in the forenoon, the wind being fair, we made eight English miles an hour; but our joy, on this account, lasted only till half past three in the afternoon when the wind, becoming a perfect gale, lashed the sea into terrible fury and caused us to expect death every moment.[1]

15th. Toward 4 o'clock in the morning of the 15th this gale was succeeded by a favorable wind which lasted till the 17th, when by 4 o'clock in the morning it threatened to change into a most furious gale. Indeed, it soon became so violent, that the Captain, who was generally a most courageous man and a daring mariner, lost his courage. So, also, did the sailors. All the sails which were hoisted were torn by the wind into tatters, and the main mast (the strongest) was broken short off. Each successive wave following the other swept over the deck or rather the ship; and so much water came into the vessel, that those who slept in the lowest bunk under the forward deck with their baggage, were flooded; and this, too although all the openings and air-holes [dead lights] were covered. Now the ship would lay on one side,

---

[1] And if not too sea-sick, Pausch probably congratulated himself on his foresight in not taking with him those " little bits of paper ! "

and now on the other — her masts touching the waters, which now rose around the ship higher than the masts. At times we seemed to be in a deep abyss between the walls of water. Every one of us, including the Captain himself, expected every moment would be our last; and each one appeared reconciled to the inevitable, giving up all hope of ever seeing America, or his fatherland again. This storm was not to be compared with those we had before encountered. It continued without abatement until eleven at night, when its fury became less. All minds were filled with fear and terror; until finally, at 4 o'clock in the morning of the 18th, the storm ceased its violence; and by afternoon, the wind became so quiet, that the vessel made no headway whatever. At 12 o'clock, the Captain ascertained, by his quadrant, that we had been driven back by the storm forty miles.

The 19th, 20th, 21st, 22d and 23d found us continuing our voyage against head winds slowly, but, on the whole, successfully. The men dried their large and small clothes by the little sun which at times shone; while, daily, the torn sails were repairing.

24th. A storm again; but fortunately not accompanied by head winds, otherwise, this one might have proved worse than the last one.

25th. The 25th was the first really fine day of our voyage since we left Spithead and the

Isle of St. Helena [Isle of Wight[1]]. All this time, up to now, in addition to storms, we had encountered very thick fog, constant rain, and very cold weather.

26th and 27th. Wind and weather good.

28th. Again, head winds. At 12 o'clock at noon, the compass showed that under the 48th degree, latitude and longitude, we were 1968 miles from Portsmouth, of which 41 was reckoned to one degree.

29th. This morning, about 10 o'clock, an artillery-man, who was doing sentinel's duty, saw land, or rather thought he saw it. Upon the fog lifting, however, and we approaching nearer, we perceived it to be an iceberg $\frac{1}{2}$ of a mile long, $\frac{3}{4}$ of a mile broad and 240 feet high without counting the 50 or 60 feet which was under water. The wind being more than $\frac{3}{4}$ a head, the ice-berg was directly in our course; and as the following night was not only very dark but foggy, had it not been discovered by us in the daytime, it might have caused a collision and the foundering of the ship. Thus, our general rejoicing at seeing, as we supposed, land, came, as the saying is, to naught. The sight of this great piece of ice so suddenly looming up at this time of the year and in such regions caused in myself and my companions (who felt

[1] See previous note.

as I did) an unspeakable yearning for a self supporting, fertile spot of land, no matter where situated![1]

30th. This day, as well as the one following, we passed on the open sea, with stormy weather and contrary winds, and suffering, withal, the cold of Winter.

31st. At noon, we were, according to our reckoning, in 48 degrees and 59 minutes longitude; and had, therefore, made 2048 English miles. The same evening, about eight o'clock, we reached the great Fishing-Banks, where we found fifty fathoms of water. Each fathom contains or is equal to six English feet.

August 1st and 2d. Our voyage was attended by head winds $\frac{1}{3}$ on our quarter. Here we caught English gold-fish.

3d. We reached the Island of Cape Breton opposite Louisburg with such a favorable breeze, that we saw Cape Race at 9 in the morning. It lies to our right, and forms with its right bank the strait or Gulf of St. Lawrence. At this point, according to the statement of our Captain and his quadrant, we had made 2103 English miles from Portsmouth, and are now in the above named Gulf.

---

[1] There must, however, have been some way of communicating with Quebec, some means of telegraphing, — since Gen. Riedesel, in his Journal, says "On the 29th of July there was a rumor that the second division had arrived after an auspicious voyage. The rumor, however, was only partially confirmed, as only one ship arrived having on board the Hesse Hanau artillery."

5th. The wind was propitious; but we could not make headway on account of the dense fog, as we had to avoid the Islands of St. Magdalene, with the dangerous cliffs by which they are surrounded, and which lay to our right. For this reason, all our sails were furled; and coming to a halt, we caught gold-fish[2] for pastime. These fish were served the next day with butter to the men as rations; and they tasted first rate.

6th. On the 6th we again had a view of the west side of this Island, which we passed at five in the evening. In consequence of the fog and the cliffs, the sails had again to be furled, obliging us to tack.

7th. This lasted till 5 in the afternoon. By four, we had in our sight the little Island of St. Paul; and on our left North Cape Breton — both of which we passed about 11 o'clock in the night.

8th. In the morning about 8 o'clock, we approached North Point passing it under a most favorable wind, at about half past eight in the evening, alongside of the West Cape or Point of the Magdalene Islands.

---

[1] *i. e.* to anchor. As a military man and not a sailor, Pausch uses the term he is most familiar with — "halt."

[2] The common salt water perch, found so abundantly in shoal water along the coast to the extreme north. They were called then, as they are now, by English sailors, "English gold finnies" and so Pausch naturally thought they were named gold-fish.— *A. McF. Davis to the translator.*

9th, 10th and 11th. Until noon, there was no wind. The weather, also, seemingly, was beautiful, notwithstanding which we made little or no progress. However, about half past twelve, we had a tolerably fair breeze, and we passed Bonaventura. At this place we sailed over a bank, where, for the distance of a mile, we had but 4 and $\frac{1}{2}$ to 5 and 6 fathoms of water. This, however, did not last long; for toward evening we found we had 12, then 15, and finally 16, and by evening, 80 fathoms of water. We rounded Cape Rosière at 12 o'clock at night, under a most beautiful clear blue sky; and early on the 12th, with extraordinary good wind, we found ourselves in the St. Lawrence, south of the Island of Anticosti. Here we met a small two master, which had on board the wives of English sailors. It hailed from Halifax; and the cargo was to be discharged at Quebec. On this ship was a pilot from the Isle of Orleans, this side of Quebec, who was engaged by our Captain to take us to that place.

13th, 14th and 15th. We reached the little Island Nicholas. In the morning, at half past eight, we were met by a large English transport having on board Royal troops from Boston; and half an hour later, we encountered four more transports, under the escort of the Royal Frigate "Pearl," carrying troops for the *corps d'armee* in the vicinity of New York. We were examined by an officer of this Frigate, who boarded our vessel from a small boat.

16th. The whole of this day, as well as the next two days (the 17th and 18th) in consequence of the untoward North West wind, was spent in loafing in the river and in tacking from one side to the other; so that we did not make a quarter of a mile headway.

Since yesterday, the mountains called Camille[1], are in sight; and if we had but a favorable wind of only $\frac{1}{3}$ on our quarter we should soon reach them. Today, we again met a Royal Frigate on her voyage. She is called the "Tartar;" and we met her about 15 miles below the above named point, close to the Camille. No officer from this frigate examined us on board, but only by a speaking-trumpet.

19th to the 26th. We reached Quebec[2] towards evening about 5 o'clock. On our way,

---

[1] There are no mountains, now called by this name, either in Canada or any where else that we know of. The mountains seen by Pausch were the Shikshock in Gaspé, with the Laurentian and Alleghany range in the distance. Possibly "Camille" may have been a local name given to them at the time when Pausch wrote, as the Agent of the Seignories, at the present day, enjoys the title of *Camille*.

[2] Quebec, which is a perfect type of an ancient medieval town, is built upon a rocky promontory, formed by the junction of the St. Charles and St. Lawrence Rivers. The highest point is on the southerly side, facing the St. Lawrence; this side is also the most precipitous and was originally about 300 feet above the water. It slopes gradually toward the north till the elevation is perhaps not more than 100 feet above the lower town. The general form of the upper town resembles a triangle, with each side about half a mile in extent, the base resting on the land side. Around the edge of this rock the wall of the city is built, which is

we met one transport with provisions; and afterwards, two frigates in succession, called respectively the " Juno " and the " Carp."

about twenty-five feet thick and twenty-five feet high, though in many places, owing to the irregularity of the foundation, it varies considerably from these proportions. The walls, having been built for defense, were constructed of course upon scientific, military principles, hence the ramparts are wanting in that architectural beauty one would see in a castle, for they are so placed that when guns are mounted upon them they may command the most advantageous positions, so that the fortification contains numerous angles, equal to almost any number of degrees.

At the time of Pausch's visit there were three gates through the town leading to the " Lower town " eastward and northward, and three leading westward out into the open country. The three former, since the garrison was withdrawn a few years since, have been razed, leaving nothing to obstruct a passage from the Lower town; the three latter still remain arched gateways, much the same, doubtless, in point of strength as when they were first constructed, but in point o. beauty recently very much improved. They are named St. John, St. Louis and Kent gates respectively, the latter in honor of the Duke of Kent, the father of Queen Victoria. Through St. Louis gate the "*grand allee*," which is French for Broadway, the broadest street in the city, leads out into the country direct to the historic plains of Abraham, which are about a mile distant. Nothing remains upon this plain to-day to tell the visitor of the scenes that were once enacted here, except a plain, round granite shaft, surmounted by a helmet, on the base of which is the following inscription. " Here died Wolfe victorious, September 13, 1759 "

QUEBEC, IN 1776.
From a contemporary Print.

At Quebec, we were ordered at once to Montreal[1] as the wind was favorable. We therefore were obliged once more to hoist anchor; and, as the wind was auspicious, sailed a little distance up the River and again anchored.

27th. During the night preceding the 27th, about a quarter to seven, we again got under way. Near Point Neuf we met a Frigate, and from her we again received an order to sail. Accordingly, we continued on, but cast anchor the same night, at half past seven, near St. Pierre.

28th. Early in the morning, at four o'clock, we set sail, and reached Champlain. Here lay

---

[1] Gen. Riedesel thus writes of Montreal at this time.

"This city is somewhat handsomer than Quebec, and may contain, perhaps, sixteen hundred houses. Its wall is nothing more than an apology for a wall with loop-holes for cannon and fire arms; and what is called the citadel is only a log house in poor condition. These works were first begun in 1736. The whole island, including the city, belongs to the Seminary. This has eleven ordained priests beside a few other priests who are distributed among the nine parishes which are on the island. These were the first priests that got foothold in this part of Canada. They came from the Seminary of St. Sulpice at Paris, and are to this day dependent upon it, having induced the king of France to grant them in 1646 this island. They have founded a very respectable college for the youth who were formerly taught by the Jesuits. Near this seminary is the best garden in all Canada. Most European plants are found here. The revenues of the seminary amount yearly to twenty thousand thalers. The few Jesuits who are in Montreal, and, indeed, throughout Canada, still own their possessions. The entire parish of La Prairie in this city, for instance, belongs to them.

"The Hospital or Hotel Dieu, in which are some members of the order of St. Augustine, is in a splendid condition. There is, also, a hospital for the army. There is, likewise, in the city a convent—La Communauté de Secours de la Congregation de Notre Dame—a general Hospital of the Sisters of Charity, and a Cloister of Recollets. Of the four churches, that of the Jesuits has ceased to exist."

Montreal was also the market place for the important fur trade with the Indians; whence the traders visited the Indian hunters in the interior, in order to exchange clothing, ammunition, ornaments, liquors, etc., for peltry.

at anchor the Frigate "La Blande;" and we were at once ordered to start for Three Rivers.[1] It was then a quarter past seven; and by a quarter of ten we lay there [Three Rivers] at anchor. The evening previous and also this morning, our ship passed over two sunken rocks and narrowly escaped being damaged.

The wheelman, the Captain, and, indeed, all of us, were greatly scared by this occurrence; for it was but a short time before this that we passed a small vessel which, two months since, had met with a similiar accident, in consequence of which she had been dismantled, and, as we passed, was lying on her side. A few hours after, we received another order to sail at once southward, with our transport, to Sorel at the mouth of the River Richelieu, across the Lake St. Pierre. The pilot and the Captain refused to obey this order on the ground that there was great danger on account of the lowness of the water, our ship drawing 14 feet; while, in some places, there was scarcely 10 to 11 feet of water.

But notwithstanding our remonstrances, the order was reiterated with the remark, "No matter how great the danger." This order was delivered by a little young gentleman of the

[1] Three Rivers, which was the head-quarters of the German troops during their winter cantonment, was the smallest of the three principal Canadian towns, and counted at this time about 250 houses with 1200 inhabitants. The chief buildings were a convent of the Augustine friars and an English barracks, capable of holding 500 men.

Mary. Now, after conducting the company thus far in safety, to imperil all merely for the sake of sailing 15 leagues farther in the same ship was absurd. Therefore, rather than run the risk of drowning, I positively refused to go further, stating that my most gracious Prince had lent the artillery company for the service of his Royal Majesty, but not for drowning purposes in the St. Lawrence River. As the distance to Montreal was but thirty leagues I took an extra post and a courier; and in the company of Lieut. Dufais (whom I was obliged to take with me on account of his knowledge of French) I started from Three Rivers a little after 3 P. M.

After traveling all night, I arrived at Montreal at half past ten on the morning of the 29th. I did not, however, meet his Excellency Governor (Lt. von) Carleton[1] for that General had made his headquarters at Chambly which is about 9 English miles from Lake Champlain. Here was the army which was divided into Regiments, and again into commands, and was encamped and partly billeted at this place. We crossed the river in small boats (canoes); thence to Chambly where I succeeded in finding his

[1] Of this General, one of the best officers, as regards kindness, justice and ability, the British Government ever had, Riedesel, in a letter to his wife, gives a peculiar picture. "In order," he writes to get an idea of his personal appearance, imagine the Abbot Jerusalem. The figure, face, walk and sound of his voice are just like the Abbot's and had he the black suit and wig, one could not discern the least difference." For an elaborate sketch of Carleton, See *Hadden's Journal*, (a work much quoted and deservedly) and *Sir John Johnson's Orderly Book*.

Excellency. Thence I went to La Prairie to call upon Col. von Gall,[1] three leagues from Chambly. Major General von Riedesel with his Regiment of Infantry and a Battalion of Grenadiers, were also stationed there. These troops, however, were posted far apart and scattered.[2]

30th. It was 12 o'clock when I arrived there; and early in the morning I reported to Col. von Gall who conducted me to Gen. von Riedesel. With these gentleman I spent the entire day.

31st. At 6 in the morning, I started for the River St. Lawrence; crossed it to Montreal; then back again to Three Rivers (traveling all night) where I arrived at half past eight o'clock on the morning of the 1st of September.

September 1st. While at Chambly, I received orders to await, with my men, the arrival of our cannon, and also the whole of their accoutrements, which were in the other ships with the fleet. For this purpose, we were to remain at Three Rivers; but upon arriving there, I found awaiting me an order to hasten to Chambly in small boats — a great number of which had already been made of pine. Leaving behind a detachment, consisting of Lieut. Dufais, 2 Bombadiers, 1 drummer, 10 artillery-men, 1 wagon-

---

[1] The commander of the Hesse-Hanau Regiment.

[2] Regarding the extent of territory occupied by the German and English troops, see note in advance under November.

maker, 5 mechanics, and 6 horsemen for artillery, and also 1 foreman for the latter, I arrived at Chambly. But I secured the above mentioned boats eleven hours too late according to my orders.

2d. It was then one o'clock in the afternoon. I began the embarcation immediately, and, with all possible speed, sailed up the river.[1] For pilots we had on each boat a Canadian. There were eight boats. My men had to do the rowing. It made no difference whether they understood rowing or not. At first, they made bad work with it; but after a while they rowed nicely. My orders were to stay at Berthier the first night, and above Sorel, the second; but this was entirely impossible. I was obliged to sail all night; and by the time the moon rose, I was on the Lake, St. Peter; and had "knocked" around in the boats for two hours between Mastriche and the River de Loup. At 12 P. M. we started once more; and keeping on nearly all day we arrived there at half past two.

3d. Here were encamped also, that portion of the 34th English Regiment which was not detached.

---

[1] This river had various names. It was called the Sorel, Chambly, Richelieu and St. John's river.

The Commander of this Regiment, Col. St. Leger[1], entertained myself and my two officers all day. His men made room for my men in a barn, where they all spent the night — a fact worth knowing by all the English and Germans in Canada. Myself, officers and men were treated with much respect and friendliness by the above mentioned Regiment.[2]

4th. Very early in the morning I gave the order to start, and arrived at 7 in the evening, or about dusk, at St. Antoine. Here my men got a barn for the night; the officers and myself going to the adjoining dwelling-house. We were received by the people here in a polite and friendly manner. Every thing — no matter what — had to be well paid for, and in cash, that the people of this province might be kept in good humor. For this reason, up to the 5th, I laid in on board our batteaux a good stock of cold meats and other ship provisions — so that the Germans, at least, might not want.

5th. An hour before daybreak, I started again, and arrived at 3 P. M., at the English camp at Chambly. All the artillery of the army in Canada is under the command of Maj. Gen. Phillips; consequently, I, too, together with my

---

[1] For a sketch of St. Leger, and the chief personages mentioned in the *Journal*, see "Sir John Johnson's Orderly Book."

[2] Lord George Germain, in a letter to Carleton, dated at Whitehall, 26 March, 1777, directs that 342 Hanau-Chasseurs be put under St. Leger for his expedition against Fort Stanwix.

company, belong here in the same camp. Accordingly, I sent forward the cannonier, Engelhard, with the letter I had with me, to our former colonel (now Brigadier General) who, with my cannonier, was to provide us with quarters in the camp already laid out.

As we had arrived here without suitable conveniences for encamping — everything of this nature being still on board the ship — Col. von Gall lent us thirty tents for the privates and subalterns. I also received from Major Williams (commanding in the absence of Gen. Phillips) two new and very serviceable tents, together with all their paraphanalia, for the use of the officers; also, fourteen new field kettles of white tin. In fact, respect and friendship are shown to us all down even to the humblest man — a circumstance which I never imagined would be the case. With the exception of not understanding the language, [we get on nicely]; but by reason of this circumstance, we are among this people like a Pelican in the wilderness.[1]

6th. I was unable, until today, to see Colonel and Brigadier General von Gall, as, before my arrival yesterday, he marched, with his Regiment, from La Prairie toward St. Johns, at which place he is to encamp. It is said that the Rebels show a disposition to move towards that

---
[1] Psalm 102 : 7.

Post. Almost the entire head-quarters of the army were here yesterday and again today ; and since yesterday, the Regiments in this vicinity have moved up the river near Chambly and are concentrating. I have just this moment received orders to do guard duty alternately with the English artillery.

7th. My officers and myself today were invited to dine with Lieut. Gen. Carleton,

8th. This afternoon, I received orders to send forward two detachments — each with an officer — one to serve four 6 pounders at St. Johns with our Brunswick Grenadier Battalion — the other to serve four 6 pounders with the Regiment von Riedesel. One marched at 7 o'clock, the other at 9 o'clock, to their destination. Lieutenant Bach goes to the Grenadier Battalion, and Spangenburg to Gen. Riedesel at La Prairie. I, alone, with one third of the Company, remain in camp near Chambly.

DETAIL.

The Hesse-Hanau Artillery Company are divided among the army in the following manner :

	Capt. Pausch	1st Lieut.	2d Lieut.	Bombadiers	Surgeon	Drummers	Cannoniers	Wagon Makers	Boss Hostlers	Blacksmiths	Wagoners	Sadlers	Hostlers'	Total
in camp at Chambly	1			5	1	2	36						6	51
Three Rivers		1		2		1	10	1	1	2	2	1	6	27
La Prairie			1	2			22							25
St. Johns			1	2			22							25
Total	1	1	2	11	1	3	90	1	1	2	2	1	12	120

We are all well except a Cannonier who is sick with the scurvy at Three Rivers. His name is Pulffer; and he is now in a fair way of recovery.

Addenda.

8th. The Regiments are gradually drawing nearer together; and some of them are advancing closer to St. Johns. Those of the boats which are completed and were on the river have mostly been transported toward Lake Champlain, which Lake is still in possession of both parties. We have two frigates on the Lake; and from all appearances, there will be a demonstration against it[2] without waiting for the arrival of the two thousand Brunswick troops, which left at the

---

[1] Or literally, "Artillery Servants." [2] *i. e.* For its possession.

same time as I did, and are destined to act with us. The Rebels are said to be strongly entrenched on the other side [end] of the Lake among the mountains, and from 600 to 1000 Savages are said to form the attacking force of the right wing. We are all on foot; and I am sorry to say that I, also, am in the same fix. We cannot get a two wheeled calash[1] — for which, too, we have to pay one shilling an hour — without trouble and asking permission of one or another general. We even have to pay out of our own pocket, the above price per hour for the small carts of the peasants on which to transport the Company's baggage, clothing and other necessary articles. This expense I hope his Majesty, the King, will most graciously consent to make up to our Company; for we cannot, as

---

[1] "The Calash," says Weld, writing of his travels in Canada in 1795, "is a carriage very generally used in Lower Canada; there is scarcely a farmer indeed in the country who does not possess one: it is a sort of one horse shay, capable of holding two people besides the driver, who sits on a kind of box placed on the foot-board expressly for his accommodation. The body of the calash is hung upon broad straps of leather, round iron rollers that are placed behind, by means of which they are shortened or lengthened. On each side of the carriage is a little door about two feet high, whereby you enter it, and which is useful when shut in preventing anything from slipping out. The harness for the horse is always made in the old French taste, extremely heavy: it is studded with brass nails, and to particular parts of it are attached small bells, of no use that I could ever discern but to annoy the passengers.

Mrs. Riedesel, also, speaking of riding in a calash, gives her amusing experience with the driver of one of them "The Canadians are everlastingly talking to their horses, and giving them all kinds of names. Thus, when they were not either lashing their horses or singing, they cried, '*Allons mon Prince! Pour mon General!*' oftener however, they said, '*Fi, donc, Madame!*' I thought that this last was designed for me, and asked '*Plait-il?*' 'Oh,' replied the driver, '*ce n'est que mon cheval, la petite coquine!*' 'It is only the little jade, my horse.'"

yet, tell whether our means, including the money for our rations, will, or will not be sufficient.

For these several reasons, I cannot take into consideration those things which belong and are essential to, position; nor, can I form an idea, until God leads me there on foot, where we shall all meet together for action. This state of affairs will certainly make campaigns — such as no man, since the existence of Hessian troops, has ever witnessed in this world! According to an old history by a certain Italian King and Campaigner, the Hessian troops had, generally, one ass for the baggage of two officers; but I am very much afraid — and the English prophesy the same thing — that in a short time, each officer will have to gird a saddle on his own back and carry his own baggage![1]

9th. This afternoon, Maj. Gen. Phillips, chief of the entire Royal Artillery in America, arrived at Chambly from St. Johns. This was the first opportunity I had had of seeing and calling upon him; on which occasion he assured me of his hearty good will and friendly feeling for my Company. We remained in camp in Winter quarters with his men and under his orders. Hence we were never with the Regiment except

---

[1] Pausch, who seems to have been not without humor, may, also, have had in his mind the last two syllables of Gen. Riedesel's name — "esel" an "ass."— The soldiers used to pun on it considerably. This fact was told me by an old officer in Germany who knew some of the officers who served under Riedesel.

when it was necessary. I ordered Lieut. Dufais to come at once, with the greater part of his command, from Three Rivers to our Camp, leaving behind a small detachment to await the arrival of the vessel containing our artillery. This detachment was then to follow.

Accordingly, I ordered the Lieutenant to leave the Artillery-man Encke in charge of the detachment which remained behind, on account of his knowledge of the French language; also, only two cannoniers with six artillery servants.

This afternoon, at 5 o'clock, I practised with the English Cannoniers firing with English cannon, and in the English fashion. It went off very well; and our firing was greatly admired by the English officers, for, with the exception of practising yesterday afternoon and this morning, this was the only time we had yet done so. Taking all these circumstances into account, I am led to prophesy good things and hope and imagine that, so far as I and my Company are concerned, we will give a good account of ourselves when the time comes. Yet I do wish most sincerely that I had my own cannons, and particularly my igniters[1] and wipers.

22d. From this time up to the 22d, I remained here in camp. We were supplied the

---

[1] Quick match-tubes.

same in every respect as the Artillery of the King, having fresh meat and very good bread.

Each day we continued our practising with English cannon and in the English fashion; and my men being ambitious soon learned the English way of firing.

The following order was received by me on the last mentioned day, viz: the 22d. It is from Maj. Gen. Philips, and it is dated, Sept. 22d, 1776.

Order.

"Captain Pausch will encamp with the rest of his Company at the Post beyond the Brunswick Grenadiers near St. Johns.

"Bloomfield[1]

"*Major the Artillery Brigade.*"

25th. This order was executed by me at once on the following day when I met [at my new post] Lieuts. Spangenberg and Bach, with four and six pound cannon. These I took with me into camp and practised with my company daily.

---

[1] Thos. Bloomfield was born in Kent, Eng., 16 June, 1744. Having entered the army, after first trying a sailor's life, he embarked with his company for Canada in the spring of 1776, and on his arrival, was at once appointed Maj. of brigade to Gen. Phillips. He took an active part in Burgoyne's campaign and was wounded in the 2d Battle of Saratoga, Oct. 7, 1777. He became a Maj. Gen. in Sept. 25, 1803, and died after a short illness at Kent, Aug. 24, 1822.

28th. I received the following order from Maj. Gen. Phillips, through the Brigadier General.

Order.

"*St. Johns, 28th Sept.*, 1776.

"Capt. Michelson[1] will embark the Companies of Maj. Williams and of Capt. Carter, in the Radeau with the 29th Regiment in addition, except the following numbers, viz:

	Subalterns	Privates
Of the Co. of Maj. Williams,	4	25
Capt. Carter	4	25
Those in addition	.	30
Total	8	80

"There must also embark on the Radeau, the Company of the Hessian Artillery except a detachment of one Subaltern and thirty men who will remain. The men must have their boots nicely arranged; and afterwards they will immediately put their cannon in position and exercise daily in the mornings and afternoons. They will, also, pay the greatest attention, so as to acquire the cannon exercise as soon as possible and in the most perfect manner. The British and

---

[1] Mitchelson. This officer did not live to see the result of Burgoyne's campaign, as he died early the next year, 1777. For sketches of Mitchelson, Williams and Carter, See Roger's notes to *Hadden*.

Hessian artillery with the additionals[1] will be divided among the cannons and howitzers except the two 12 pounders which will be placed one on the prow and the other on the stern. These latter will be served by the Hessians, and will be under the charge of Capt. Pausch, and his two subalterns; ten privates to each cannon.

"The officers for the Radeau[2] will be the following, viz: Maj. Williams and adjutant, Capt. Carter, Captains Michelson [Mitchelson] and Hermann, Lieutenants Houghton[3] and Cass, with the three newly appointed Lieutenants, and the subalterns of the 29th.

"Also Capt. Pausch and two of his subalterns whom he may designate for that purpose.

"There will also be embarked one detachment from the 29th Regiment who are to act as Marines. The officers should know that in the present condition of affairs they should not encumber themselves with much baggage or many 'traps.' The service will be severe; but the

---

[1] The 29th Regiment.

[2] "The Radeau (named 'The Thunderer') was an unique structure which is often mentioned in the naval annals of the northern lakes. It was square built and scarcely more than a raft or floating battery, but constructed with great solidity and strength. It was protected only by low and slight bulwarks, but armed with the heaviest ordnance; and was a powerful and effective craft." It carried 300 men.

[3] William Houghton was at this time fire-master, having been appointed to that position the previous July. The duties of this office, says Gen. Rogers, was to attend to *the making up of all kinds of ammunition*; whether for practice or service; and if there was a laboratory he had charge of it, and was accountable for all tools and materials used therein."

Major General has the greatest confidence that the Corps will maintain their honor, and at the same time, the dignity of their respective commands; and that they will act with the greatest zeal and courage while in the service of His Majesty.

"BLOOMFIELD,
"*Major of Brigade.*"

"Major General Phillips will issue the order designating the time of the embarcation: meanwhile, Capt. Pausch will have the goodness to give out provisions for two days, at the same time, stating what the men shall take with them when they embark.

"BLOOMFIELD"

I carried out the above order the same day, and, embarking in small batteaux, reached the Radeau the same evening. I found it already crowded with men, so that there was room for no more. All the Englishmen, on account of this overcrowding were unpleasant companions. There was no room even for our baggage. Accordingly, I sent it all back, the same evening, to Montreal in a wagon accompanied by the head hostler. I, also, in fact, sent all the hostlers with the cannonier, Bauer, back to Montreal, with instructions to remain there until further orders. As it rained very hard, I was obliged (in order that some of my men might have rest and be dry) to station on deck a strong guard which was relieved alternately.

29th. The following day, an arrangement was made by the Captain in command, whereby all those on duty were relieved in regular order. To facilitate this arrangement, I always not only furnished an officer, but often took his place at night, in order that he might enjoy a night's rest.

There being no wind at this time, the Radeau had to be drawn ahead by the men in this way, viz: a heavy anchor was sent far in advance in boats and lowered into the Lake. A strong rope was then put through rings and pullies; and thus, the Radeau was moved ahead. This worked splendidly, especially if the wind was not unfavorable. The Radeau, at the same time, formed the headquarters of the ammunition and provisions.

October 1st. I only remained here till the 1st of October, when I received the following Order from Bloomfield.

Order

"*St. Johns, Oct. 1st.*

"The Radeau not having sufficient room to contain all the people that are on her, the men will disembark on the *Isle aux Noix*[1], and re-remain there until receiving a new order.

"Capt. Michelson [Mitchelson] will likewise encamp with his detachmeut upon the *Isle aux Noix* (during the time that the Radeau remains there) placing on board one officer. To the Artillery will be assigned eight batteaux which will accompany the Radeau for the purpose of carrying their baggage. These batteaux will each have a guard of two men of the 29th Regiment, and one Canadian as a pilot. The Detachment of the 29th Regiment, acting as Marines, will likewise have four batteaux for their baggage.

"BLOOMFIELD."

"The Major General has appointed Mr. Harow Superintendent of the Sailors in the armed batteaux; and they will be under his command, and obey his orders.

"Two batteaux, with the two cannon and their ammunition for the Hessian artillery, will be under the orders of Capt. Pausch.

"B."

---

[1] A small island in the River Sorel, nine miles from St. Johns. It is well fortified and commands the intercourse by water between Lake Champlain and the River St. Lawrence. The early explorers found on the Island an abundance of walnuts, hence the name.

7th. 8th. But they did not arrive on the 7th, but on the afternoon of the 8th. We were all in readiness to embark; and, in the course of an hour, Lieut. Dufais and myself started with two baggage-boats. Before starting I provided my detachment with fourteen day's provisions, consisting of *Zweibach*[1], salt meat, etc. I was, however, obliged to leave behind, Lieut. Bach, 3 subalterns, 1 drummer, and 22 privates, for nearly all of them were sick with the dysentery. Lieut. Bach, whose conduct and zeal in the service were of the right metal, requested permission to accompany us; but I could not grant his request, for he was really very ill with that complaint, which fact he sought to hide from me. There was on this Island before we arrived, an English artillery Captain, named Jones, who pretended that the command of the artillery had been given to him. Unfortunately, however, for his pretensions, at the time he said he had received the command, he was crossing the Equator on his way to the East Indies.[2] Lieut: Spangenburg remained behind at this place with a detachment and baggage-boat, to wait for the arrival from St. Johns of an armed batteau which was expected. For this reason he was left be-

---

[1] Burned or toasted biscuit; a very favorite article of food with the Germans even at the present day.

[2] Pausch, who evidently tries in general to be just, allows his prejudices to prevail in speaking of this officer, who was one of the most meritorious in the British service. Rogers, in his *Hadden's Journal* thus speaks of him.

"Thomas Jones entered the Royal Military Academy at Woolwich as a

hind. I left with him the order, as soon as the batteau arrived, to sail at once without delay, be it day time or night time, and at any time he pleased: also, if there were no wind, then to row. This order he carried out with the greatest accuracy.

On the 7th the following note was written me from St. John's.

"A batteau with one piece of cannon together with its munitions and equipage, for the Hessian Artillery, under the order of Captain Pausch, [will be sent forward]"

gentleman cadet, March 18, 1755, and was commissioned a lieut.-fireworker in the Royal Artillery Dec. 27, 1755; a 2d lieut. April 2, 1757; a 1st lieut. Jan. 1, 1759; a capt.-lieutenant Oct. 23, 1761; and a capt. Jan. 1, 1771. He served in the 1st Battalion until he got a company, when he was transferred to the 4th Battalion. He took part in the siege of Belleisle on the coast of France in 1761, and proceeded with his battalion to America in 1773. He was stationed n Canada in 1775, so that he was in America long prior to the arrival of the artillery detachment that was sent out in the spring of 1776. The artillery present at Quebec at the time of Montgomery's attack, and during the subsequent siege of the town by Arnold, belonged to No. 3 Company, 4th Battalion, but they were very few in number. They were under the command of Capt. Jones, whose services on the occasion received the highest praise. In the operations to expel the Americans from Canada in 1776, Capt. Jones took an active part and was attached to the right wing of the army. In the autumn of that year he returned to England, and on the 31st of the following January was married to a Miss Ibbetson, of Greenwich, at St. James Church, Piccadilly, London. He returned to Canada in the spring of 1777, arriving at Quebec early in June with a company of artillery, and that year participated in Burgoyne's campaign on which he was attached to Gen. Hamilton's Brigade in the right wing of the army. Lieut. Hadden was attached to his company and has given us *post* an interesting account of the almost complete annihilation of Capt. Jones' company, and of the captain's death at Freeman's Farm, Sept. 19. Stedman in his 'History of the American War,' in speaking of the artillery in that engagement, says, — 'The intrepidity of Capt. Jones of the British artillery, who fell in this action, was particularly distinguished.' Lieut.-Col Kingston, Burgoyne's adjutant-general, in testifying before a committee of the House of Commons, speaks of Capt. Jones as "a very gallant man,' and Gens. Burgoyne and Phillips, in their reports, give him conspicuous mention."

But this note, with the expected batteau, did not arrive at the *Isle aux Noix* until as late as the 10th. Under it, Capt. Jones, commander of the artillery, had written as follows :

"Mr. Spangenburg, Lieutenant, will set off for the army with this batteau with as much expedition as possible.

"Given at the *Isle aux Noix*, 10th Oct. 1776, at 9 o' clock in the morning.

"*Thos. Jones, Capt Br. Ar.*"[1]

A few days later, Lieut. Spangenburg arrived at Crown-Point, bringing with him two of my missing batteaux containing equipage and provisions, and also ten Hauau soldiers. The third one, commanded by Bombadier Wachter, was still missing.

The Radeau, under a favorable wind, made such good head-way that I was unable to catch up with it.[2]

I should have said that on the 9th I reached after dark River la Cole, where I met His Excellency, Gen. Burgoyne, with an English Brigade of Infantry, to whom I reported and also delivered letters.

---

[1] See note on Thos Jones, *ante*.

[2] The Radeau, we are told by Hadden, once sailed under a favorable wind, from Crown-Point to *Isle aux Noix* (90 miles) in 9 hours.

10th. From this place I started before daybreak, and reached the Radeau at a Point[1] far beyond Point au Feu in the real Lake Champlain.

11th. We raised our anchor, and, with favorable wind, got very early under sail. At 5 o'clock in the morning, we received orders to get in readiness for an engagement. About half after ten, we heard the sound of artillery; and soon after, under a splendid and auspicious wind, all the batteaux met the enemy's ships in a bay behind an island. The first sight, encountered by our advance guard, was a frigate of the enemy stuck fast on a stone cliff or island and abandoned; and soon after we saw two other frigates sending forth a lively fire. Besides this they had several armed gondolas, which, one after another, emerged from a small bay of the island firing rapidly and effectively. Every once in a while they would vanish in order to get breath, and again suddenly reappear.

Our attack with about 27 batteaux armed with 24, 12, and 6 pound cannon and a few howitzers became very fierce; and, after getting to close quarters, very animated. But now our frigates approached. One of them, the "Maria," having His Excellency, von Carleton on board, advanced

---

[1] Probably Wind-mill Point.

and opened a lively cannonade. This one was replaced by the frigate "Carleton;" and as she in turn retreated, the "Inflexible" took her place only to retreat as the others had done. One of the enemy's frigates two of which were at *echelier*, or rather at *echelon*, one behind the other, began to careen over on one side, but in spite of this continued her fire. The cannon of the Rebels were well served; for, as I saw afterwards, our ships were pretty well mended and patched up with boards and stoppers.

Close to one o'clock in the afternoon, this naval battle began to get very serious. Lieut. Dufais came very near perishing with all his men; for a cannon-ball from the enemy's guns going through his powder magazine, it blew up. He kept at a long distance to the right. The sergeant, who served the cannon on my batteau, was the first one who saw the explosion, and called my attention to it as I was taking aim with my cannon. At first, I could not tell what men were on board; but directly, a chest went up into the air, and after the smoke had cleared away, I recognized the men by the cords around their hats. Dufais's batteau came back burning; and I hurried toward it to save, if possible, the Lieutenant and his men, for, as an additional misfortune, the batteau was full of water. All who could, jumped on board my batteau, which being thus overloaded, came near sinking.[1] At this moment, a Lieutenant of artillery by the name of Smith, came with his batteau to the rescue, and took on board the Lieutenant, Bombadier Engell, and one cannonier. The remainder of Dufais's men, viz: nine cannoniers and nine sailors remained with me; and these, added to my own force of 10 cannoniers, 1 drummer, 1 Sergeant, 1 boy and 10 sailors — in all 48 persons — came near upsetting my little boat, which was so over-loaded that it could hardly move. In what a predicament was I? Every moment I was in danger of drowning with all on board, and in the company, too, of those I had just rescued and who had been already half lost! It being, by this time, nearly evening, the batteaux retired. The Radeau arrived at dusk because, although we had a favorable wind, it was light, and it made, in consequence, but little headway. Any way, the two 4 pounders did their best, in firing at the frigates of the enemy. The distance, however, was too great, so that no ball was effective, and the approach of night prevented our advancing nearer. This night a chain was formed of all the batteaux; and every

---

[1] "Of the Germans," says Gen. Riedesel, "Lieut. Dufais of the Hesse-Hanau Artillery, distinguished himself on this occasion. He was in command of an armed sloop carrying a 12 pounder; and although he was hard pressed by the enemy, and his vessel finally sunk, he yet fought so desperately as to succeed in saving his gun and bringing it to the vessel of Captain Pausch. Two of his men, however, were drowned, and he barely escaped a similar fate." In this connection see Gen. Riedesel's account of this Naval Battle, in which he gives full credit to the Hesse Hanau artillery.

one had to be wide awake and on the alert. The Captain's frigate, which had run aground, was set on fire at dusk by the orders of his Excellency; and her ammunition, blowing up, caused a fine fire lasting all night. Up to this time, nothing more occurred; for the enemy's frigates remained in the same place where they had acted on the defensive. Toward morning, however, it was clear that they had escaped. A pursuit was begun and some vessels were captured. Five large and small vessels, which had entered a bay on the left shore were set on fire and abandoned by the enemy. The following night, my batteau, together with some other armed English batteaux, lost sight of the fleet on the Lake; and we were thus forced to continue rowing by guess-work the entire night, that we might not be left behind. The next morning at daybreak, we were lucky enough to meet a few English vessels which had met with the same experience as I had. Others followed in my rear, so that I arrived in time (ahead of some and behind others) at 9 o'clock A. M. at Crown-Point.[1]

23. From this time forth, a chain was formed every night across the river[2] with the batteaux

[1] By comparing Pausch's account of the action on Lake Champlain with that of Gen. Rogers in his Sketch of Arnold in his *Hadden*, the reader will see how exactly Pausch tallies with Rogers. In fact, these two accounts of this famous action must ever, henceforth, remain as *the* authorities on this subject.

[2] Pausch calls this portion of Lake Champlain "The River," as the Lake narrows considerably at this point, becoming narrower and narrower till it forms Wood creek. The chain extended across from Crown Point to Chimney Point almost directly opposite on the Vermont shore.

from which some thirty were detached for this purpose. Between 10 and 11 o'clock in the forenoon the men would row to each shore where they cooked and ate — returning before sunset to their respective positions and casting anchor.

On the 19th Inst. Gen. Phillips sent me, by an officer, the following order .

"*Crown-Point*, 18*th Oct.*, 1776."

" Monsieur :

" Maj. Gen. Phillips directs me, on his behalf, to signify to you his entire approbation of the brave conduct of Lieut. Dufais and the subalterns and soldiers of the Hessian Artillery who took part in the attack upon the Rebel fleet, the 11th of this month, under your orders. He begs you to accept his good wishes and his best acknowledgments; and that you will be assured that he will always remember it.

" I have the honor to be very sincerely, Monsieur, your very humble and very obedient servant.

"Thos. Bloomfield,"
"*Major of Brigade.*"

" To Captain Pausch."

Meanwhile, there was no scarcity of provisions. Each man received plenty of salt meat. *Zweibach*, and Rum. They made acquaintances among the Indians, and traded with, and bought of them fresh mutton and beef. So that the officers and privates lacked for nothing — that is, if we except the former who were partly in need of tea and coffee, wine and other drinkables.

During our last engagement, Lieut. Dufais lost one cannonier named Rosemer who was shot dead, and the drummer, Pillant, and the pilot, who were burned up. A sailor, also, lost his leg by the same ball that killed the cannonier, and which dug a hole under the gun-carriage three inches above water-mark. During this time, all ate and drank rum and water together — officers as well as men; and for a change, water and rum! Salt meat and *Zweibach*, continued to be our food.

24th. In accordance with an oral order, I disembarked my men and encamped near the left wing of the 29th English Regiment, by this means relieving an English officer with his detachment, of whose cannon, with their necessary equipments, I took charge.

27th, 28th. I also received the following order from Gen. Phillips:

"*Crown-Point, Oct. 28th,* 1776.

" Capt. Pausch, with the detachment of Artillery under his command, will break camp to-morrow morning and embark his company upon the four batteaux destined to join those now upon the

River.¹ They will descend the Lake as far as the *Isle aux Noix,* where he will take the detachment of his company (the same as those at St. John's) and will return to Longville [Longueil] which place he will make his quarters until new orders reach him to take up his winter-quarters at Montreal.

" BLOOMFIELD."

28th. After 9 A. M., I embarked in the above mentioned batteaux on my return, and arrived the third day — traveling all this time alone — at the *Isle aux Noix.* I was alone as the wind and weather, generally, had separated me from the other batteaux. Three nights I spent on small Islands and reefs, where the wind and waves had cast me; continually in the open air and near the fires which we had built. On the third day (as I have said), I arrived, under a most favorable but high wind, at the *Isle aux Noix* — only an hour after Lieutenants Dufais and Spangenburg. Here I gathered up all that were left — those who had not died or who were not in the hospital — in six batteaux, and, the same day, reached the camp near St. Johns. I was determined to make this voyage while the wind was favorable.

31st. For want of carts, I was obliged to remain till towards noon. Finally, by dint of hard

¹ See previous note.

work, and with the assistance of Maj. Barness (commander of the Brunswick Battalion of Chasseurs) I procured them, and reached La Savanne[1] after dark, over a wretched and nearly impassable road. Here we found some houses in which we took up our quarters.

Nov. 1st. I arrived at Longueil by way of La Prairie. I occupied at this place good quarters; and, on my giving a receipt, I received from a Captain of the Militia residing here fresh bread and fresh meat for the first time, except when at Crown-Point, where I had received the same for a few days for my command. The same day, I traveled with Lieut. Sartorius to Montreal. I met the latter at La Prairie, having had occasion to call upon him in reference to procuring money for the payment and transportation of the troops.

Here I met Col. Leutz, Capt. von German, Capt. von Geismar, and von Schoel (a convalescent) and Lieut. von Boetzig, who had been ordered to this place. All of these gentlemen started, with the baggage left at Montreal, a few days later, for Berthier, where the Regiment had already gone into Winter-quarters.

---

[1] La Savanne does not apply to any town (as might be inferred from the text,) but means a low, swampy district. Such as lies between La Prairie, Longueil, Chambly, and St. Johns; from which low land Montreal is, at the present day, supplied with the best of hay." *Letter from Mrs. L. J. A. Papineau of Monte Bello, Canada to the translator.* Riedesel dated several of his letters to his wife from this district.

7th. This evening, I received by an officer sent expressly, the following order from General Phillips:

"*St. John's, 7th Nov.,* 1776.

"Captain Pausch, with the company of Hessian Artillery, will proceed to the fields at *Point aux Tremble,* where he will encamp until the barracks at Montreal are in a condition to receive it. He will take his orders from Brigadier Gall regarding the workings of his Brigade, which will be attached to his [Pausch:] Company during the winter, in order that all may be collected together; and that there may be no farther change in the orders upon this subject.

"BLOOMFIELD, *Maj of Brigade.*

"*N. B. Point aux Tremble* is situated in the Island of Montreal almost opposite Longueil."

Early the next morning I ordered the general *reveille* to be beaten: and half an hour later we started. Lieut. Spangenburg, Tour, and Schutzen I dispatched [in advance] at 6 in the morning to the Quarter Master General (Capt. Money) at Montreal, with orders to provide quarters. As I was on the point of starting with the company, I received from the Quarter-Master General the following letter:

"*Montreal* 8*th Nov.,* 1776.

"SIR:

"I have the honor to inform you that the barracks will be ready next Sunday; and, if you judge best, your company can start Sunday at whatever hour you please; or if you prefer to start to-morrow and march to *Point aux Tremble*, you shall have the necessary batteaux and carts.

"Yours,
"*J. Money*,[1]
"*D. Q. M. Gen.*"

9th. This news obliged me to return the following morning and reoccupy my old quarters.

8th. On the 8th, the lost gunner, Woehler, with five more cannoniers and the servant of Lieut. Spangenburg, made his appearance.

On the 6th, Cannonier Scibold died of dysentery on a small Island (the name of which I do not know) and was buried there. I questioned Bombadier Woehler why it was that he had been so long absent? He stated, that after loosing us, he had drifted about on the Lake — the waves casting him first on one island and then on another—until, finally, when he had about given up, he fell in with some Canadian

---

[1] John Money, we are informed by Rogers in his *Hadden*, was born in Norwich Eng., about 1740. He accompanied his regiment to Canada in the spring of 1776, and as we see by the text, took part in the operations against the Americans that year under Gen. Carleton. The next year he accompanied Burgoyne on his expedition as Dep. Quarter-Master Gen. After being precipitated from a balloon into the sea and being nearly drowned, and passing through many other adventures, he died at his seat near Norwich called Crown-Point, (Did he name the place to remind him of his American Campaign?) 26 Mar. 1817. He became a full General, June 4, 1814.

batteaux and canoes, by the aid of which he succeeded in reaching the *Isle aux Noix*. Thence he traveled to St. John's by water, and from there overland, he reached Longueil. Here he found my order and procured a cart. I rejoiced from the bottom of my heart to have these poor devils back again. During all this time, they had met with nothing but misfortune; and, indeed, I had given them up for lost. Fortunately, they had with them the provisions intended for Lieut. Spangenburg's detachment (except the rum); and thus, being not in danger of starvation, were enabled to sustain life for a time. Lieut. Spangenburg and his men were provided for by us. My company had allotted to it six large rooms in the barracks with fireplaces; and to my subalterns were given two rooms. All Captains of Artillery, including myself, are billeted in the city. Each room, occupied by my men, contains ten beds — every bed holding two persons. Every Saturday, wood, coal, and lights are distributed among them from the magazine; and, on every eighth day, provisions are dealt out to them fairly and equitably. Nearly all the winter they were furnished with fresh meat and very good bread. Each man, with the exception of those who are sick, draws salt beef and pork, and very good butter. The latter article is served out at the rate of one pound per man for eight days; and every time that salt meat is given out, pease and oat-meal are also furnished. For all this, the company have to thank solely the kind care of Gen. Phillips, who is just as solicitous concerning our rations and treatment as if they were the Royal Artillery — composed of his own men. Immediately upon going into our winter-quarters,[1] the entire company, by order of the General, were furnished with the following articles of winter clothing. Each man then, received the following articles, viz :

One pair of long blue cloth over-alls such as are worn by sailors, which come high up above the hips and way down to the shoes. These are fastened under the feet with a leather strap, and have five buttons on the outside of each leg and

---

[1] The winter-quarters of the Germans were in and around Three Rivers, as far down as Chambly, on the western side of Lake St. Pierre, and between the St. Lawrence and the Richelieu. The more special divisions were as follows : The regiment of Specht as far down as Champlain, near Three Rivers, and the place called Batiscamp ; the regiment of Rhetz from the last named place to Fort St. Anna. These regiments sent off detachments to the parishes south of the St. Lawrence. The dragoons and regiments of Riedesel were quartered in Three Rivers. Two squadrons of the former, and three companies of the latter, had the town assigned to them. The two other squadrons were transferred to Cape-de-la-Madelain, the two other companies to Point-du-Lac. The regiments were also obliged to send detachments to the nearest parishes on the other side of the St. Lawrence. The regiment of Hesse-Hanau was removed to the parishes of Berthier and Masquinonge. It, also, sent out detachments to oocupy St Francois and Sorel. The regiment of Prince Frederick occupied the parishes of Riviere-du-Loup, and Machiche. The grenadier battalion was quartered in St-Charles, St. Denis, and St. Tours. Barner's light infantry was sent to Buloville and Chambly, where it was joined by the company of sharp-shooters. The artillery of Hanau was quartered in Montreal. The amount of territory occupied as winter-quarters by the German troops was much too large for the number of men. Those of the Brunswickers, for instance (only 2,282 in all), occupied a front of no less than thirty-three German miles.

extend about a quarter the way up from the ankle, also :

One large blue woolen cap.

One pair of blue mittens lined with corduroy material.

One capacious under-jacket, the sleeves being made of strong white corduroy. One Canadian over-coat with a cape and facing of white sheeps wool, and bound with a light blue braid. The cape itself is made out of a whitish gray cloth[1] a kind of melton. It is bound with light blue woolen ribbon, and in three places extending down in front to the waist it is fastened with rosettes — these latter being made out of this same blue ribbon. This garment is called throughout all Canada a *capot*.

For this entire outfit the following sums were deducted from each man of the company.

	a.	p.		
In September			5 shillings	no Pence
" October			5 "	"
" November			5 "	"
" December			5 "	"
" January			5 "	"
" February			5 "	"
" March			3 "	9
Total			33 shillings	9 Pence

[1] The word which I have translated "whitish gray," conveys to a German exactly what we mean, in speaking of the color of a cloth when we say "pepper and salt."

This was the cost including the making.

Each of these suits costs about 3 shillings less than those furnished to the English artillery; and for the reason, that I, myself, saw to the making of them up even to the smallest detail — had it all done, too, in Montreal, and made all the bargains myself. There was another reason, viz: Among the English artillerists are the tallest, strongest, and handsomest men in the world. Consequently, it required more material of each kind, than it did for my men.

The blue cloth and the corduroy are already on hand; for as I was too far away from Montreal to attend to the purchase myself, I had it bought in that town at the same time as was that of the English artillery which has just returned from St. Johns. Immediately upon receiving it I paid the commissary for it in cash, taking his receipt.

These outfits — so necessary in this part of the world — are of great service to my men, especially those who are sick. Of the latter, there are over thirty who are suffering from a kind of scorbutic itch.

Indeed, I have been, from the start, the most miserable and unfortunate of all the commanders of the German Companies. Each of my men who was sent to the Hospital was not only afflicted with dysentery, but, as the hospital doctors told me, talked day and night of fathers, mothers, brothers, sisters, cousins, and aunts — besides, also, talking over and repeating all kinds of German village deviltry — calling now this one, and now that one by his baptismal name until they had to stop for actual want of breath! For this disease there is, as is well known, but one remedy in the world, viz : dear peace, and a speedy return ; and with this hope I comfort my sick daily. With those still alive and well, I am perfectly satisfied ; for they find plenty of solace in the Canadian girls and women. For this reason, and in their companionship they are happy and contented.

After making the necessary arrangements for the preservation and quiet of the sick, I asked the General for an order to enable me to bring my cannon, carts, harnesses, &c., from the River Sorel to Montreal. This I did that I might ascertain how many were left, and in what condition every thing was — so as to be prepared for actual service.

16th to the 29th. I made this request in writing and in the French language ; and, on the 29th, received the necessary order enabling me to carry out my purpose.

The river was still open ; and accordingly I embarked in four batteaux, taking with me

Lieut. Spangenburg, the servants of the company and all the men necessary. The same day we reached *Point aux Tremble* — distant from here two and one-half leagues.

30th. I remained over night at La Valerie, where I met Capt. Schoell who, with his company, were quartered in this Parish.

Dec. 2d. 3d. I reached Berthier, the head-quarters of Col. von Gall, and, under the supervision of Lieut. Spangenburg and wagon-master Zicklamm. I had everything transferred from the transports to ten batteaux, and had them taken to Berthier by way of the River Sorell and across Lake St. Pierre. I also arranged everything with Lieut. Sartorius regarding the balance of the pay due us from November.

4th. I had the freight of the batteaux equalized; and, with the consent of Brig. Gen. von Gall, had given orders to start the next day at sunrise, when, toward 9 o'clock, the same evening, I received another order from him directing that everything should remain in *statu quo*, as he hoped that my company, also, would go into winter-quarters at Berthier on the *Isle au Bas*.[1]

---

[1] Evidently some mistake in spelling on the part of the writer, as, in this connection, *Isle au Bas* has no meaning in French.

5th. Consequently, I had everything taken from the batteaux, re-landed, and collected together near head-quarters. Those articles which required to be covered I stored in barns.

6th. I sent my men on batteaux to La Valentine, at which place they remained over the night.

8th and 9th. Late in the night I returned to Montreal. I had not strictly carried out the order of the General to whose Brigade I really belonged, and, indeed, still belong ; and I thus, innocently, met an offended gentleman and sour faces. I explained to him, as well as I could, that not only my Instructions but my letter directed me to place myself under the orders of Brigadier von Gall. Upon this statement, Gen. Phillips immediately wrote to Gen. Carleton, the commander-in-chief at Quebec. As a result of my letter it was decided that the Hessian Company of Artillery should go into winter-quarters with the English in the same barracks and there remain.

Jan. 22d, 1777.[1] Our cannon and all the baggage and acoutrements arrived towards evening, having been transported overland with horses by

---

[1] It will be observed that there is here an interruption in the Journal extending over forty-four days of December and January. From the fact that it was the most leisurely period of winter-quarters ; and also from the additional circumstance that Pausch was in the habit of transmitting his daily records—either the first draft or a copy — to Prince William by every opportunity, it is natural to suppose that either his notes are lost, never having reached their destination, or that they may be still extant (but not yet discovered) in Hessian manuscript collections public and private, and may yet turn up when least looked for.

the Canadians. They were brought into the Barrack-yard, where they yet remain.

23d. The birth-day of the Queen was celebrated; and a salute of seven cannon was fired three times at the Citadel. My cannon were used for this purpose — there being no others here.

The 29th Regiment and the English Artillery marched in front of the Citadel. The former fired three salutes from their muskets after every seventh cannon shot. Each cannon was charged with fully three pounds of powder — a charge which these cannon had never before contained. This, as I understood it, was intended as a test of the strength of the guns. Since then, whenever the weather is favorable, I have the men drill daily according to our established method. They are improving considerably — the greatest part of the men taking interest in the drill.

I must say that, in some respects, I am fortunate in having my Quarters in the barracks at Montreal, and not in an extensive Parish; since I can thus take care of the sick and the well. Besides which, having my men close together, I can easily correct any thing that needs a change. In the country, for instance, with my men scattered singly among the inhabitants of the shanties, I should have lost half of my young men; and being separated from the English Artillery, they would not have received half of the care and attention.

Every one was obliged to be at Parade at 11 o'clock A. M.— the English Artillery as well as my own. The companies formed in line at the barracks and were taken by companies to the Parade Ground. They were obliged to run sometimes for a half, and sometimes for a whole hour.

This came the harder on my men as they had never been drilled in it before. However, this exercise (which they were obliged to practice continually) was very conducive to their health. They had, also, to dress themselves properly every day; to comb and powder their hair: the more so, as the General, himself, inspected them man and man.

March. My bat,[1] baggage and forage money goes at such a rate, that I actually don't know where it goes to. I had to furnish each of my men with four good undershirts, two new outside shirts, with two pair of linen coverings for the arms, two pair of shoes, and new stockings for nearly all. This I must do, if they would appear properly. Besides this, I had the misfortune to lose my chest containing 47 pairs of new white pants, and 49 pairs of new white leggins. I had them replaced by new

[1] Money for the pack-horses.

ones, and distributed among the company. Most of the pantaloons are of fine bleached twilling; for I could not obtain strong linen white enough. The leggins cost, each, 30 French *aunes*. About 60 Hanau yards cost 16 piasters, equal to 44 florins.[1]

In fact, the entire outfit costs $\frac{5}{6}$ more here than in Hanau, when I can buy everything for $\frac{1}{6}$ less than it costs here. Shoes and leather are here, also, excessively dear, as are all other necessaries no matter what they are. I had rather have a *Sechsbatschen*[2] in Hanau (for I can do more with it) than a piaster here, which, in Hanau money, is 2 florins and 36 kreutzers.

April. All the officers have to add money of their own, or else live poorly. A bombadier, for example, has to pay for a pair of boots 20 florins; for a pair of leather pants 20 florins; for a coat, five times as much as in Hanau; and everything else in the same proportion. Why, a bottle of the poorest red wine costs, in our money, 36 kreutzers, and a bottle of Madeira 1 piastre!

For the last three weeks we have had orders to hold ourselves in readiness for marching. St. Johns is the place of *rendezvous;* and it is also the arsenal, and the main depot for our ammuni-

---

[1] One florin — equal to 37 cents or $\frac{1}{8}$ English money.

[2] A coin of the value of four silver groschen, equal in our money to twelve and one-half cents.

tion and provisions. All our fleet (both small and large vessels) are anchored there. Everything, it seems, is to be taken from there in batteaux to the *Isle aux Noix* — that is, after the army has broken up and left their winter-quarters. We will then occupy our old post of Crown-Point, which we captured last year, and thence, we will undertake an expedition against Carillon[1] or Ticonderoga. It is rumored that the enemy's fleet is at this place — though under not very auspicious conditions. It is also said, however, that the fort at Ticonderoga — so far as regards situation, garrison and cannon — is strongly fortified.

Regarding the charges against head-smith Brads concerning discipline, service and insubordination, the Brigadier General will send in his reports and protocols. I wish to gracious that I had never seen such a "cuss;"[2] also, I hope never to see another one like him. I fervently hope that he will sit in chains in a London jail--for this is all he is good for in this world. There is no more despicable beast in this world than he. He respects neither God nor his Superiors. This is the second time that he has been confined in jail — having been, now, over two months in Berthier — where I have sent

---

[1] A chime of bells. So named by the early French, on account of the music of the waters.

[2] The exact translation.

him to be tried by a court-martial of the Regiment.

On the 5th of March, at 7 A. M. I ordered out my Company for inspection, near the Quebec Gate at Montreal. They were closely examined on this occasion by the Inspection Commissioners, the Captains of Artillery, and by Adj. Gen. Foy[1] — which inspection took about half an hour. The latter (Foy) paid me a compliment after the muster — saying that he was greatly pleased, and that he would report the satisfaction he had experienced to His Excellency, General Carleton. He left us the same day; and a few days later, I learned from a letter from the Brigadier General that he had expressed himself to the same effect at Berthier.

The Muster-Roll, attested by the Commissioners and sworn to, I immediately sent to Berthier; and I trust that it arrived there at the same time as that of the Highland Regiment.

---

[1] Edward Foy accompanied the Brunswick troops from Germany to England, and thence to Quebec, where he arrived June 1st, 1775, having gone to Canada as commissary of the troops there. He was appointed Dep. Adj. Gen. to the army in Canada June 3d, 1776, and Adj. Gen., June 6, 1777. Gen. Burgoyne wished to have Foy join him on his expedition, but Sir Guy Carleton who was about to return to England could not spare him. Foy was appointed Secretary of the Gov. Gen. of Canada, July 1st, 1778; and he died April 27th, of the next year. Foy's wife accompanied the Baroness Riedesel to Canada in the spring of 1777, when both ladies went to join their husbands. The Baroness, in her journal, however (see Stone's *Memoirs of Madame Reidesel*), gives anything but a flattering description of her traveling companion. For a more detailed account of Foy, see "*Hadden's Journal*" annotated by Gen. Horatio Rogers.

On the 11th of March, the entire English Artillery and also my company were reviewed by His Excellency, Gen. Carleton, and Gen. Riedesel. After the review and while yet in the Parade ground I received a notification, by an Adjutant of Artillery, that the General-in-Chief was highly satisfied. Soon after, I had the same sentiments from Gen. Riedesel in an Order of Gens. Carleton and Phillips expressed in good German. Regarding this Review, instead of the so-called Muster-Roll, a Report is attached and hereby annexed under L. K.

April. For this campaign, the *douceurs* for the Bat-baggage[1] and forage money, according to the list made out the 11th of February, for the past year, were received excepting for the doctor, Wagon-Master and the foreman of the hostlers—of whose pay (by order of the Lieut. Gen. and Col von Gall) one half was kept back — that is, 6 Livres (8 Florins 9) total 19 Livres,[2] which was paid to Lieut Sartorius — and for which, a receipt was taken.

Closed the 20th April, 1777.

G. Pausch.

---

[1] *i. e.* Baggage on the pack-horses. [2] 6s. 3d., English money.

Continuation of the Journal — interrupted April 20th, 1777.

28th. After getting my package ready to send, I heard by chance, that Gen. Phillips intended to send despatches in haste to Quebec, where a vessel was said to be on the eve of sailing down the St. Lawrence to the open sea for London. As I was anxious to profit by this opportunity (for which I had so long waited) to forward my Reports and my Journal with six plans besides other things, I begged, at the next following reception of said General, both as a particular favor to myself, and more yet, as a gracious attention towards my Master, His Serene Highness, the Prince, that he would send my package under cover of his mail and with his best recommendations to London. To this request he consented without hesitation. Accordingly, upon the day appointed by him for this purpose, I did not fail to hand to his Secretary my package securely sealed; and I fervently trust that it will reach the hands of His Highness without the least delay, and even quicker and more securely than my former one.

May 15th. Between my last date and this, I did not fail modestly to present the following points :

1st. I sent a Report in regard to the condition and real effective force of the command graciously entrusted to me.

2d. There was ordered for the English artillery long, loose, and wide linen overalls — such as the Sailors wear — to be made in one piece from one end to the other; and to be of the same length as leggins. They were mostly made of old tents. I found this kind of clothing to be very well adapted to this climate and our present situation. They were particularly convenient not only for marching, but as a protection against the insects[1] which are especially annoying to the men both in the field and in the camp. Lieut. Dufais and myself amply tested the merits of this clothing last year, while on our journey to and from Three Rivers and Chambly. As the Artillery were obliged to do duty in this kind of uniform, and as it made a good impression generally, and promoted harmony when it was seen that we were willing to wear them, I determined to adopt the dress. Accordingly, as I had no old tents which would serve the purpose, I did not hesitate, but bought, at the lowest price, Russian linen and had it made up into pants. I intend to deduct the actual cost of this clothing from the pay of the Subalterns, Musicians and Cannoniers in two payments, and for this reason, viz: that the

[1] Mosquitoes?

pants are, like their winter clothing, an article which cannot be paid for out of the fund devoted to sundry small prescribed articles of dress, having no connection with them. These pants are now all finished, and are worn by the men not only in the barracks, but when off duty and at drill.

For the last three weeks I have drilled every morning from 6 to 8 o'clock, after the lately introduced fashion — with only one Company. In the afternoon, two of my cannon are served by the English, and two by men from my Company when [ball] cartridges are used. I, for one, never am present but send my officers instead — for the reason, that only an English captain is sent there, and only an English officer commands them on these occasions.

The National pride and arrogant conduct of these people allow them to command *my* men, while I am not permitted to command *theirs!*

I lately requested Gen. Phillips that he would furnish me powder for my own drill. This request he at once granted. This was at one o'clock. At three o'clock, it was countermanded through the influence either of the Major or some one else. Jealousy was the cause of my not being allowed to drill separately any longer ; and I was thus forced to drill at 4 o'clock in the afternoon, according to their orders and by their drums, which my men do not understand at all, and who, if I left them to drill alone, would be totally demoralized. In fact, the Devil of Jealousy has been aroused because the English see that my men drill quicker and more promptly, and because, also, the spectators do us the justice publicly to acknowledge this to be the case. Hence, instead of the former friendship between us, there is now enmity. They imitate our Artillery in different things, as, for example, in the matter of our wipers — of which they are having some made for their 3 and 6 pound cannon. Every day, to my disgust, I have to practice the [lately] introduced quick-step, which we do not have, nor do they have it in Prussia — nay not in the world, except in the chase, with fast horses and good dogs! This is a splendid exercise for the men in winter; but in the summer, when the weather is warm, it is detrimental to the health of the men. It has no good result except to make the spectators laugh — for by this manœuvre no closed ranks could be kept in an attack upon the enemy. In case, therefore, of a retreat we would not only fare badly, but would be exposed to the well deserved censures of the European and American press.[1]

There is a daily parade from 10 to 12 o'clock — frequently to 12:30 — and every evening, from 5 to 7. Every man in our service must turn out

---

[1] The Press was a power even in those days!

and be present. Having anything but a full Company, and having, at times, from 10 to 12 men sick at the barracks with the bad, and in this country, the ever prevalent diarrhea, I send two officers. The General daily assumes more and more authority — encroaching more and more upon our jurisdiction.

The head-smith, Brads, was sentenced by Court Martial to two months imprisonment on bread and water as a punishment for his wickedness and excesses. This will be fully shown by the documents which will be submitted by Brig. Gen. and Col. von Gall. A few days after the sentence, his fascinating daughter called on the General, and his wife on the Major. As the result, I immediately received an order, through Lieut. Dufais whom the Major met, at once to liberate the head-smith, Brads. I immediately obeyed this order, but, at the same time, reported the fact to Brig. Gen. von Gall. Thus both his authority and mine were at once overthrown, over which circumstance the English and Brads, himself, crowed loudly. It was pretended by the latter [*i. e.* the English] that the work of the blacksmith was needed; but this was only a pretext, for, from the beginning, I had substituted Cannonier Walter, a thoroughly good mechanic. The King's work, therefore, would not have suffered; for two blacksmiths are all that are required.

That number is all that is allowed me; consequently, I have no right to have more.

Brads states in public that being, at present, in the service of the King and in that of no other, no one else has authority over him; and this statement has, of course, [as things are] many supporters. I wish I were entirely rid of him; and that I could give him up to his protectors; for I fear that there will yet be a terrible scene with him the first time he transgresses, in the least, the rules of respect and discipline. I am sure of this, for I know that certain matters of jurisdiction are reserved in the treaty which was ratified by his Majesty, the King.

I also add two copies of a protocul regarding Cannonier Nantz who is now in jail and guarded by a watch. An English officer had him arrested and brought before his Main Guard, and afterwards cast him into prison without informing me. He was afterwards taken from prison and brought into the Guard-room, where the commanding officer of the Guard, by the name of Williamson of the 29th Regiment, after cuffing and kicking him, sent him back to the jail — a place, where we, at home, put only pickpockets, highwaymen, murderers and assassins.

The circumstances of the case are as follows:

Cannonier Nantz was called a " Dutch bugger" by a man wearing an overcoat with a hood (as all soldiers and inhabitants hereabouts do), and leading a girl by the arm. Expecting anything but such an epithet from a soldier or even from a Canadian peasant, Nantz answered. "*You* may be an infamous bugger, but what am I doing to you, you dog, that you should call *me* a bugger?" Suddenly, a glistening bayonet appeared from under the cape. Nantz, a good, brave soldier, and as decent and as resolute a man as there is in the Company — and not intoxicated as he had left his bed in the barracks only three-quarters of an hour previous — draws his sabre. Hesitating, however, to use it, he strikes, with the flat side of the blade, the head of his antagonist just as he was in the act of using his bayonet. But the sabre glancing off, he cuts one of his cheeks; whereupon the man with the overcoat runs away!

Nantz quietly pursues his way to the barracks; but while in the act of passing the Guard, he is drawn in, arrested, and maltreated in the manner just mentioned. To his question " what crime he had committed?" he is told that he had struck this officer. Whereupon, he replied, that he had not known he was an officer; that he was heartily sorry for it; that he never supposed that an *officer* would call him a " Dutch bugger ;" that, as he had said, he had not supposed him to be an officer, but had taken him to be either a rude soldier or a Canadian peasant; and, finally, that the Prince, whom he served, had not a single "bugger" in his service, but only brave soldiers as good as they were themselves — and that they all served the same King.

On the following morning, I received an order to investigate the case. This was on a Monday, and also a tea-party day.[1] I took with me my three officers as assessors. The aggrieved officer, who could only speak English, came also accompanied by a corporal of the English Artillery who spoke German. I had the accused brought before me and close-questioned him. Meanwhile, the officer confessed that he had called Nantz a "bugger." "Why?" was my question to the officer. "Because," he replied, "the cannonier had looked at him." "Now," I asked the cannonier, "Why did you look at the officer?" He replied, that "he had served his Majesty, the King of Prussia, for eight years, and was allowed to look at him whenever he met him; and, moreover, he had never been reproved for so doing; that he and every one else had a perfect right to look at any one whom they met in the public street."

Perceiving, therefore, that I could do nothing in this matter, and that the whole affair would result unfavorably before the officers, I sent him to my Guard-House.

[1] That is, a reception held at stated times by the Generals and their wives.

While at the Court Tea-party, I received from Major Gordon[1] of the Engineer Corps (who, during the presence of Lieut. Gen. Carleton was vice-commander) an order to deliver the "wretch" to the Main-Guard, which I did. A few hours afterwards, I received another order to take a receipt for the " wretch " from the Main-guard, and keep him until further directions. Three weeks went by without any further enquiries regarding the case.

Meanwhile, a spy enquired of my officers if the cannonier was in jail or on duty? I answered that he was on duty since no other order had been received respecting him. The General, also, asked me in the drawing-room, the

---

[1] Harry Gordon of Knockespock, in the parish of Clatt, Aberdeenshire, came from an old Scotch family, that obtained from James IV, in 1508 a grant of the barony of Clatt, which was renewed by James VI, in 1604, " to his beloved James Gordoun of Knockespoke." The early British Army Lists do not mention the Engineer Corps, so it is impossible to state when Major Gordon entered the Royal Engineers. In the Army Lists of 1756 he is down as a sub-engineer, which grade was equivalent to a lieutenant of Foot, but no date of commission is given. He became an engineer in ordinary and captain Jan. 4, 1758, and a major in the army July 23, 1772. He was serving in Canada in Sept., 1776, and he had probably been stationed there for several years prior thereto. A letter written from Quebec, to be found in the *London Chronicle* for Aug. 7-9, 1777, says, "Major Gordon, Chief Engineer, goes home, and is succeeded by Capt. Twiss of the same corps;" and the same paper for Aug. 5-7, 1777, under date of Aug. 6, says, " Col. Gordon, lately arrived from Quebec, was presented to the King at St. James, and had the honour of a conference with his Majesty." He became a lieut. colonel in the army Aug. 29, 1777, and a sub-director of engineers and major in that corps Dec. 18, 1778. His last promotion was Nov. 20, 1780, when he was made a colonel commandant of Engineers, or simply colonel, as that grade afterwards was known, and his name appears in the Army Lists for the last time in 1787. He married a Philadelphia lady named Hannah Meredith, by whom he had four sons and two daughters, and one of his sons subsequently became a major-general in the army. His descendants still survive. [*Hadden's Journal.*]

same question and received the same answer. Finally, he wrote to the Brigadier General for the Judge Advocate. The latter arrived. The officer was to be summoned; but it was said that he was sick in quarters at Longueil, but would put in an appearance in three days. But he came not. At length, it was determined that the examination should begin. I asked for and procured an English officer who could speak German. The investigation began. It was translated into French and submitted to the General by the Major. At the close of the investigation I was asked by the Major why I did not pronounce sentence on my man? I answered that "they should first examine the officer; and then I would leave it to himself to say whether or not the prisoner was guilty."

Lieut. Dufais was accosted in the courtyard at Head-quarters, (where I would not go) by the General and questioned about this case. The latter was forced to acknowledge that he had reason to be perfectly satisfied with us in every respect so far as regarded our duty; but, in this particular case, "we should," he said, "have entered a complaint; for it was not gracious, neither was there any occasion to take satisfaction into our hands." In reply, Lieut. Dufais wanted to know "against whom we should enter complaint? for, among so many people, we could not know the officer who assailed our man : and that it would be ridiculous to complain of any one, by chance, without knowing the offender : also, that these affrays occured a hundred times in this place between the men [*i. e.* yours and ours but who could tell the names of those who run away like boys!!" Now, however, there is trouble all around; and we still remain in disfavor with the General, on account of the talk and remarks there have been concerning this affair.

The General said, he would have the case investigated. We answered, that it would be impossible, if conducted in the English language. If, however, they had no confidence in a Court-Martial composed of officers of the Hanau Regiment, there was a German General of the Brunswick troops here, who would certainly investigate the matter impartially. This proposition seems on the point of being accepted, and appears to meet with approval. In view of this, a note has been sent to his Excellency Gen. Carleton at Quebec: and His Excellency Gen. Burgoyne, and Gen. Riedesel will be here in a few days, so that the case may then, possibly, be decided.

Maj. Williamson got it into his head that he could order me to forbid my men going out in the evening with their sabres. But I told him that I would not dare receive such an order from any one except my Gracious Prince, and therefore I could not obey him : further : that should I meet any one of my men either during the day or at the time for retiring at 9 o'clock, going to his quarters without his sabre, I should have him flogged the next morning. I further said, that it was a standing order at our Capital, where four or five battalions were collected at a time, that no soldier in uniform should be without his side-arms.

Since then, I have never been asked to do this; and in fact, it would fare ill with my men were such an order enforced — since were they to depend on boxing for protection, some would return to Germany cross-eyed and some blind!

The most friendly feeling and unanimity exist between the Royal Artillery and the subalterns and privates of my Company. This state of affairs I am endeavoring to maintain and foster with the greatest care and particularity.

My powder-flasks are all warped in consequence of the dampness of the batteaux and the wretched weather; and they cannot be repaired in this place.

The General, who lately examined the arms of my Company, said that he finds the carrying of catouches very cumbersome and hard on the men The General is right; especially as regards the piece of wood attached. I told him I had already sent an humble statement, regarding this very thing to my Prince, and hoped to be able to discard the powder-flasks; but if the General desired it, I would have the cartridges attached to the white straps. The first day, he merely alluded to it. The next day, he spoke of it again, saying, I would do well if I could free the men from this piece of wood. I was very glad to have the suggestion, for the wooden contrivances were not at all ornamental, and, on account of the expense, I could not procure new ones, although the old ones had become warped out of all shape. I, therefore, had the cartridges fastened to the belts until such time as I should have further orders from his Highness, the Prince — which will come in the future. They are now the prettiest cartridge-pocket one can see or wish for. They look very nicely on the men who have now entirely destroyed the catouch-boxes.

17. In the afternoon, His Excellency, Gen. Burgoyne, and staff arrived here.

18. A Reception was held to welcome him at half past twelve. It was then and there, that the Major General and chief of the Royal Artillery in Canada, with great condescension, praised the Company entrusted to me, for its appearance, discipline and the service rendered. He also praised the Company for its fine cannon-drill;

and introduced Lieut. Dufais and myself to the members of his staff. The [my] other two officers, whom he had not introduced because they could not speak French, were presented by one of his adjutants who spoke good German. His Excellency was very gracious and expressed his gratification at the good report made of us by Gen. Phillips. He gave us also the assurance of his future good will.

17. I received an order, dated May 17th, 1777, translated from English into German.

Maj. Gen. Phillips received the following order dated " Head-quarters at Quebec, May 10th, 1777, from His Excellency and Commander-in-chief Gen. Carleton.

" His Majesty, the King, has graciously determined to send on an expedition a Detachment of the army, under the command of Lieut. Gen. Burgoyne, to consist of Grenadier and Light Infantry from the following Regiments, viz: the 24th, 9th, 20th, 21st, 47th, 53d, and 62d. Fifty men from each of the above specified Regiments are to remain behind.

" Of the German troops, a detachment of Samaritans[1] to the number of 650 men, in the same

---

[1] Not quite clear. However, as the Germans use the term " Good Samaritan" as we use it, it is very probable that the word is here used to designate the Hospital Guard. Pausch, as we see by his Journal, often expresses himself with considerable originality, and it would be just like him to use this expression for a hospital guard.

proportion, will also remain behind. The first named corps is to hold itself in readiness to march upon receiving the first order from Lieut. Gen. Burgoyne, from which time, all reports are to be made to Gen. Burgoyne as Commander-in-chief. The Detachment, consisting of the fifty men from the above mentioned Regiments, together with 1 Captain, 2 Subalterns and inferior officers— in the proportion as set down for each Regiment will rendezvous at the Head-quarters of their respective Regiments, and will remain there until further orders. The Artillery with its staff, the General Hospital Department, and the Commissioners, are to send in at once a Report stating whether or not they are supplied with every necessary for a campaign.

"Capt. Foy,

" *Adj : Gen.*"

Respecting that miserable rascal and head-smith, Brads, I received the following order, dated the 16th of May, 1777.

" Sir:

"It seems a very extraordinary proceeding to hold under arrest for many months, a soldier for the sake of punishing him, as, by this means, the particular service, for which he was destined, will suffer greatly by his detention. It is very likely that this was not contemplated by the

Treaty, that a soldier should receive pay and provisions, and yet not render any service while under employ.

"I cannot interfere in this affair; and I have accordingly, given orders that the Smith shall be liberated according to the wish of Brig. Gen. Gall: and in making use of his services, you will do with him as you and the Brigadier shall judge the most proper.
"Montreal, May 16th, 1777.
    "W. PHILLIPS,
        "*Major General.*

"*P. S.* You will have the goodness to make a Report of this to the Brigadier."

It being post-day, when I received this, I sent the above order in the original to Berthier to the Brigadier General, saying I waited his orders as to what I should do in the premises. The General left it with me whether or not to have him re-arrested. I left him, however, undisturbed, as he was in the employ of the King—saying I would first await orders from my Chief at Berthier. At the same time, I gave it as my opinion that the fellow had already been somewhat punished; and as I did not wish to belittle the General, the wretch had better be released from further punishment, and allowed to continue at his work.

In time of war, I find sentences of this kind out of place, as long, that is, as the offence is not a criminal one. Prompt punishment — such as running the gauntlet, whipping, or confining in fetters for a time — is the best that can be done on these occasions, as by these light punishments, the service does not suffer.

19th. Brought to a close, the 19th of May, 1777, in the Winter-quarters at Montreal. It looks, now, as if we were on the point of starting [on the Expedition]; and, perhaps, we will really do so before the end of the month.

Continuation of the interrupted Journal, which was forwarded [to Germany] from Montreal.

21st. A grand Review was held by His Excellency, General Burgoyne, who arrived here, on the 17th, from Quebec. The Review consisted of all the Artillery here in garrison, which is composed of three Royal Companies and my own. It was similar to the one held here last Winter by His Excellency, General Carleton.

For this reason, I forward with this an appended Report of Gen. Phillips, signed by me and marked " L. A. ; " one by His Excellency,

Gen. Burgoyne, signed by Gen. Phillips; and one by Major Williams, also signed by myself.[1]

At the close of the Review, Gen. Phillips, through one of his adjutants, expressed his gratification at, and his thanks for, the valuable services rendered by my Company from the first hour to the present time. He also ordered these sentiments to be stated to each man of the Company individually. I immediately complied with his wishes, so far as the officers were concerned; and the latter in turn, announced it to the men. After this had been done, the General delivered a long address, in the English language, to his own Artillery, which, so far as I could make out, was nearly of the same general tenor.

This Review was held on the Heights behind the Fauburg de Recollets, and continued from 10:30 to 12:30. When it ended, the Company returned to their Barracks.

23d. The Review of the 29th Regiment was held at the same place. This regiment was in garrison here this Winter; and, it is said, will remain in its present quarters for the entire year. As yet, all is quiet in this garrison.

30th. The Grenadiers and Light Infantry, who were in Winter-quarters here [Montreal]

---

[1] This Journal as before observed, was written for the eye of the Prince of Hesse-Hanau; and was forwarded to that personage from time to time, as an opportunity occurred.

have started to-day on their march down to the River Sorel. At the present time of writing, it is rumored that their destination is as far as Chambly, St. John's and the *Isle aux Noix*, where the advance-guard is to await the coming of the main army — after which it [the advance-guard] is to march further on.

28th. Last Wednesday, the 28th Inst. an Artillery company (the one of Capt. Wachers) belonging to the advance-guard, marched in the same direction, viz : the River Sorel, and, thence, will go up the River. As it is still impracticable to transport our baggage over land, we will very likely have to make use of the two rivers for our advance.

June 3d. As I have just now ascertained from Capt. Gerlach of the Engineers, all the German Regiments have broken up their quarters and have started for Sorel, whence they will be conveyed on batteaux further up the Sorel River to their place of destination.

May 30th. I received the following orders :

First Order.

"His Excellency, General Burgoyne, directs that, without exception, no officer shall take with him any more baggage than he is in extreme need of. The officers are, therefore, ordered to deposit their baggage where it will be safe.

"The officers of the English Artillery offer to take charge of the equipage of the officers of the Hessian Artillery with their own. By the express orders of General Burgoyne, no more than three women can be taken with each company."

The other order relates to the Infantry, and has, therefore, nothing to do with the Artillery.

June 2d. SECOND ORDER FROM MAJ. GEN. PHILLIPS.

"*Montreal, June 2d,* 1777.

"The British Artillery will set out next Thursday for Longueil; and the Hessian Artillery will be prepared to set out Friday, the 6th, or Saturday, the 7th.

"CLIELAND.[1]

"*Lieut. and adj.*

"*Royal Artillery.*"

On the 30th of May, His Excellency, Lieut. Gen. Carleton and Suite also arrived here from Quebec.

---

[1] Samuel Cleaveland, Lieut. 7th Reg. of Foot, March 26th, 1773; Col. Artillery, Oct. 30, 1775; Capt. in the 16th Reg. of Foot, May 24th, 1776.

4th. This being the greatest holiday, viz: the birth-day of his Majesty, the King — a salute of twenty-one guns was fired from the citadel. The 29th Regiment of Infantry, here in garrison and which turned out on the *Champ de Mars*; three general detachments of the English Artillery also stationed here; together with my Company, marched to the citadel and paraded in honor of the day.

At the close of this military display, the higher officers, namely, his Excellency, Carleton, Burgoyne and Maj. Gen. Phillips, with their staffs, repaired in a body to the citadel. There, at their order, the English gunners charged a six pounder with one of our style of wipers, first with blank cartridge[1] then with ball. These wipers, and the manner in which they were handled in working the cannon, met with approval; and they will, in all probability, be adopted by the English Artillery in Canada. During the salute, Maj. Williams asked me to come to his quarters at 5 o'clock this afternoon both to receive orders for our march, and to learn of the arrangements made for our transportation. It is now a quarter past three o'clock; and in an hour and three-quarters I shall find out what I wish to know, and be able to add it to this day's Journal.

[1] Literally "blind wipers."

At 5 o'clock, I received no further orders, excepting that a trial of minute-firing would be held at the citadel in presence of the whole body of Generals with a 6 pound English cannon, only 4 feet, 9 inches long (Kass[1]), and served by English Artillerists; and also with one of my cannon 5 feet, 11 inches long, worked by my men.

The English managed to fire eleven times, and my men twelve times (*N. B.* After each discharge the gun is spunged out). If I could have omitted the wiping, which during minute-firing, is never practised, and kept right on firing, as it would have been the proper way to do, I certainly could have fired nineteen to twenty times. But as the other side started the thing, I could not possibly avoid doing the same. They have introduced the custom of dipping the wiper in a bucket of water under the cannon. This, however, is of no advantage, as it only increases the dampness, and, after a while, causes a tough gum to form inside of the gun which adds to the labor and retards the firing. I know by experience how the "Chevalier Pfalz[2] Artillery" for a long time used this precaution, more detrimental than useful — Since it caused accidents which were only avoided after

---

[1] Kass, an abbreviation for Cassel. Meaning by Cassel measurement—as the foot, as well as other measures, vary in Germany according to the district.

[2] Electoral Palatinate.

the custom had been done away with. The custom has, therefore, been abandoned [by us] years ago, in fact more than twenty.

I have, also, advised those here — by whom I could be understood — to give the practice up; but whether my well meant advice will be heeded or not I do not know.

Shortly after this exercise, the above mentioned Generals sent the English Artillery Adjutant, Lieut. Clieland[1] to me with their compliments. At the same time, they expressed their entire satisfaction both at our Artillery itself, and at the manner and agility with which our cannon were handled; and, as they wished to introduce the same method, they desired me to give and to cause to be given all necessary advice and assistance, in order that their artillerists might also be enabled to work as well and as rapidly as mine. This latter request, I respectfully promised to fulfill; the more so, because, a year ago, they were very kind to my Company in showing us their methods of loading and handling the cannon

5th. The remainder of the companies of the English Artillery who were here in garrison, having gone by way of the St. Lawrence to Longueil, and who will go thence to our place of rendezvous at St. Johns, I shall be left behind

---

[1] See previous note.

till we meet there. The time for me to march is now set down for the 8th or 9th of this month, when I shall go to Longueil, and there await the necessary authorization papers to march, by way of La Prairie, to St. Johns. There is no doubt that these strong, well formed men, who look as if they had been picked out of an army, will, in a short time, learn, and do as well and even better than my small but very attentive, willing and excellent men ; for the former, according to their fashion, have great ambition, more so, indeed, than the rest of the troops.

Last evening, the 4th Inst., all the houses in Montreal, and in the suburbs of Quebec, St. Lawrence and Recollet, were illuminated, on account of its being the greatest National festival, viz : the birth-day of his Majesty, the King ; and each citizen had a *feu de joi* [bon-fire] in front of his dwelling. There was continual gun and pistol firing from sunset till one o'clock the next morning. Those who did not illuminate their windows were in danger of having them broken by stones; consequently, those houses which were not illuminated were few and belonged to those who were too poor to do so, for they certainly were not Rebels.

7th. In the evening I received the two following orders from Maj. Gen. Phillips :

"*Montreal, June 7th,* 1777.
"*Captain Pausch: Commander of the Hesse Hanau Artillery.*

" You will start with the company of Hesse-Hanau Artillery from Montreal on Tuesday, the 10th inst, crossing the River at Longueil. You will march, also, on the following day, to Chambly and St. John's. At this latter place, you will receive four field cannon, which will form, under your orders, the Artillery Brigade, and which will be attached to the left wing of the Army. The orders, concerning this matter, have already been sent to Maj. Williams.

"You must see Lieut. Barmer, Asst. Quarter-Master General, in order to have some boats for the transportation of your baggage to the other side of the River; and for carts, you will have to apply to Maj. Gen. Duprés, who will furnish you with all you require both for the service, and for repairs.

" The Artillery of Hanau, consisting of three field-cannon, are to be left at Montreal under the command of an officer who is to take charge until he receives other instructions. You will, also, take such things with you as you need and may particularly desire; and, if you think it best, two carts of ammunition.

"Meanwhile, the officer has to report for orders to Col. St. Leger, who will determine what orders shall be at once given.

"*Dated at Montreal June 7th.*

"W. PHILLIPS, MAJ. GEN.'

"*Montreal, June 8th,* 1777.

" Dear Sir:

"As it is not entirely certain that the Chasseurs, who are expected to arrive from Europe, and are destined for the secret expedition under the command of Col. St. Leger, are from Hesse-Hanau,[1] and as the Regiment of Hesse-Hanau may not send off any detachments hired for that purpose, do not send any detachment for service. It is the opinion that the Artillery Company of Hesse-Hanau, under your orders, will embark with the Expedition under Lieutenant General Burgoyne. You will, therefore, move with all the companies of Hesse-Hanau (as previously advised) on Tuesday the 10 Instant. The cannon must be left in charge of an officer

---

[1] The result, however, proved that the Chasseurs did come from Hesse Hanau. According to Col. Rainsford's " Journal as Commissary for embarking foreign troops in the English service for Germany," three companies of Hanau Chasseurs sailed from near Dort, April 16, 1777, for Canada. One of these companies, consisting of 342 men and all of them trained riflemen, was in St. Leger's Expedition — detailed for that purpose by Carleton acting under the orders of Lord Germain.

who will take care of them, following the first instructions he received from Montreal.

"*To M. A. Capt. Pausch.*"

The other order which I received at the same time, was as follows :

" Dear Sir :

Lieut. Col. St. Leger is the Commander of an army corps, to which will be attached a body of cavalry, which, they say, are Hessians. These latter are expected to arrive shortly and are to go upon a secret Expedition.[1] It is therefore necessary that two cannon be added to the cavalry on their arrival, as they are ordered to follow the route of Lieut. Col. St. Leger in conformity with the instructions they will receive from him. You will, accordingly, have to give your orders for one officer, two under-officers, and sixteen artillerists of Hesse Hanau, who are to await the arrival of the corps of cavalry, in order to join them and receive the instructions of the commanding officer. You are also to see to it, that two pieces of Hanau Artillery, with 200 charges of ammunition for each piece, (in the proportion of two thirds round-ball and one-third of cartridges for the Artillery), are provided — also, every thing necessary for repairs on the way.

---

[1] This body of cavalry either did not arrive in time, or the order was countermanded, as no cavalry were with St. Leger in his expedition.

You will, likewise, give the order who is to take charge of the Artillery, and hand it over to the commander of the cavalry on his arrival; and you are also to order twenty-four (24) soldiers to be attached to the same Artillery, and to provide for every thing which this corps may require."[1]

The army smithey is at St. John's. Two of my ammunition-wagons and all of my cannon, with the rest of the Artillery, are at Montreal. At the same town, also, are the chests of the officers and all the stores of clothing. I left wagon-master Kaiser and an artillery-man in charge. We are using English cannon.[2]

Concerning the Action of the 19th of Sept. 1777, on Freeman's Farm near Stillwater on the Hudson River.

Sept. 19th. On the morning of the 19th of September, 1777, the entire army, with th exception of the Regiment of Hesse-Hanau which formed the rear guard for the protection of the artillery and baggage, began a forward move-

---

[1] There is no signature to this last letter; and there seems to be some confusion, also, in the dates of the letters, as under the "7th," Pausch receives a letter dated the 8th, I give the text, however, exactly as it is in the original.

[2] There is here again a break in the Journal until the actions of the 19th of Sept. and the 7th of October, 1777. This is probably caused — not by the missing portion having been lost, as may have been the case previously, but by the fact, that the writer had no time to continue the Journal; as he was continually on the march from this time until those battles.

ment.[1] The batteaux, also, followed along the Hudson with the provisions.

The disposition of the march was the same as on the 17th, viz: in two columns: the one on the right [under Fraser] consisting of the Royal troops, penetrated the mountains and woods, roads and paths: the one on the left, took the plains along the Hudson.[2] Presently, we came across a demolished bridge over a swampy ditch.[3] After a short halt, during which the bridge was in the least possible time repaired, we resumed our march, which, however, was of brief duration; for in a little while we encountered another demolished bridge, which we also had

---

[1] This advance began from "Sword's House." The site of this house is on the south bank of a spring brook, about fifty yards west of the Hudson river, and a few rods north of the south line of the town of Saratoga. It may be readily found from being about thirty rods north of a highway leading from the Hudson river road westerly, which highway is the first one north of Wilbur's Basin. This highway was nearly the same at the time of Burgoyne's visit in 1777, as it is now. It is on land now owned (1886) by a Mr. Chase, about three miles south of Schuylerville. All traces of it are now obliterated, save a pile of brick, and a slight depression in the soil where was the cellar. A son of the Sword who owned this house, and who was born at Fort George, Saratoga Co., N. Y., became a bookseller in New York city; and his tablet is still to be seen in Trinity Church, New York City. Those of our readers who are interested enough in this subject to follow *Pausch*, should consult "The Military Journals of Gen. Riedesel," and "Burgoyne's Campaign," where every step of Burgoyne's progress is described and annotated in full.

[2] There were really *three* columns, Fraser took the extreme right on a ridge (here spoken of as "the mountains"); Burgoyne, the centre; and the Germans under Riedesel — including, of course Pausch's Artillery — the " plains along the Hudson;" or, more properly, the river-bank.

[3] This bridge was over the creek that ran into the Hudson at a place now (1886) called "Wilbur's Basin." At this time it was quite a large stream, but having since been diverted into the Champlain canal it is at present only a muddy ditch. The land in which this is (1886) owned by a Mr. Hoag.

to replace by a new one.[1] While thus engaged, we heard firing in the direction of our right wing. It was then about one o'clock in the afternoon. At first it was musketry, but soon we heard cannon also. This firing soon attracted our attention by its rapid increase; and Gen. Phillips, who was with our column, hastened at once to the right wing for the purpose of accelerating its march. Soon after he had gone, Gen. Riedesel detailed two companies of the Regiment Rhetz, under command of Capt. Von Friedendorf, to a hill in front and a little to the right of us, which they occupied, at the same time reconnoitring the *terrain*.

The picket of our right wing had met the advance-guard of the enemy;[2] but the latter being superior in numbers, caused our pickets to fall back under the protection of their advancing column. This incident was the beginning of an engagement, which, in a short time, grew into a stubborn battle. Gen. Riedesel sent one of his adjutants with orders for his own Regiment to march with dispatch to the scene of conflict; it being his intention himself to place the men in position. Scarcely had this Regi-

---

[1] This second bridge was about 1,500 feet from the bridge just mentioned (Wilbur's Basin) and fifteen feet north of the first canal bridge south of Wilbur's Basin. Its site is now occupied by the Champlain canal. This point is an important one, from the fact that it was the *extreme southern* limit on the river bank, reached by Burgoyne's army in his expedition.

[2] Under Morgan.

ment marched, when another adjutant of the General arrived with the order to send him two cannon. Everything being quiet in front of our left wing, I started with two cannon, ammunition and a cart containing shovels, picks, etc., etc.

Leaving Lieut. Dufais with the cannon and baggage, and giving him the necessary instructions, I hastened up the hill, where I found the above mentioned regiment. I placed my cannon in such a position that I might be enabled to use them advantageously in case of need. The General, before my arrival, had made use of two companies of the Regiment Rhetz for the protection of the right wing of that regiment, by making them construct a hedge of branches and trunks of trees, etc., etc. He also sent Lieut. Reislin, with a small detachment, to a hill in our front, sparsely covered with trees and brushwood, with orders to give timely notice in case the enemy showed signs of occupying it. For this purpose, he was to send out patrols; and in case of being attacked in force, he was to fall back on his regiment. In the mean time, we were to keep perfectly quiet in our first position.

The General, at the same time, sent a subaltern, with four men as a patrol, for the purpose of establishing communication with those who were in action, that he might the more easily march to their assistance in case of necessity.

The first not returning, he sent a second and again a third in rapid succession, fearing that the first patrol might either have lost its way or been destroyed.

The firing seemed to draw nearer; from which one might infer that our right wing was retreating. Accordingly, without waiting longer for the report of the patrols, which had not yet come back, we left our position, and marched for about a quarter of an hour in the direction of the firing. We then formed in line of battle, I placing the two cannon in the road which led into the woods. The fences, which lay to my left, I had already quickly thrown down in order that the enemy, on his approach, might not hide behind them. This was our second position.

Meanwhile, Major von Geismar, who was yet on the staff of Gen. Riedesel, was sent by the latter to see if there was any possibility of reaching Gen. Burgoyne and informing him that he stood here in readiness with his own Regiment, two companies of the Regiment Rhetz and two 6 pound cannon, and that he was only waiting for orders to reinforce him. In the meantime, the patrols returned one after the other. The second patrol having reported that the communication between us and the troops in action was open, the General [Riedesel] marched at once toward the right.

He choose this way, in order to make a division on the right flank of the enemy. He also ordered the march to be beaten on the drums, which caused the men to cheer repeatedly. After descending the hill we met von Geismar on his return with orders from Gen. Burgoyne directing Gen. Riedesel to attack the enemy on their right flank, and, if possible, to follow them up. This, however, we were prevented from doing both by the woods and the swamps behind which the enemy were hidden. I was also to go to the right wing of the 21st English regiment.

My wagon-master, who was now well mounted, was sent ahead to find a way through a cornfield, that we might avoid the ditches and swamps and not get stuck in them.

Under a shower of the enemy's bullets, I safely reached the hill just as the 21st and 9th Regiments were about to abandon it. Nevertheless, I continued to drag my two cannon up the hill, while Gen. Phillips exhorted the English Regiments, and the officers their men, to face the enemy. English captains and other officers and privates and also the Brunswick Chasseurs, which happened to be detailed here, grasped the ropes. The entire line of these regiments faced about, and by this faithful assistance, my cannon were soon on top of the hill. I had shells brought up and placed by the side of the cannon; and as soon as I got the range, I fired twelve or fourteen shots in quick succession into the foe who were within good pistol shot distance.[1]

The firing from muskets was at once renewed, and assumed lively proportions particularly the platoon fire from the left wing of Riedesel. Presently, the enemy's fire, though very lively at one time, suddenly ceased. I advanced about sixty paces sending a few shells after the flying enemy, and firing from twelve to fifteen shots more into the woods into which they had retreated. Everything then became quiet; and about fifteen minutes afterwards darkness set in.[2]

[1] Gen. Riedesel in his memoirs, pays the following tribute to *Pausch* at this critical period of the action. He says: "when Gen. Riedesel arrived at the eminence [the hill up which Pausch also had clambered] the battle was raging the fiercest. The Americans, far superior in numbers, had for the sixth time, hurled fresh troops against the 20th, 21st and 62d Eng. regiments. The guns of this wing were already silenced, there being no more ammunition and all the artillery men having been either killed or wounded * * * Meanwhile, Captain Pausch, arrived with his guns at the right moment, and forming into line with the English, opened fire with grape shot. The Regiment Riedesel also arrived at the nick of time, and joining the two companies on the ditch [*i. e.* those from the Regiment of Rhetz already sent forward] considerably extended the line of fire."

[2] There can be no question that the day was saved to the English or rather that they were kept from a most disastrous defeat, solely by the timely arrival of Riedesel with his men and the cannon of Pausch Fraser, who was a witness of this, in a journal circular to all the English Generals, gave the fullest acknowledgments to the German troops: and yet Stedman — considered by many and among them the deservedly high authority, Gen. de Peyster — *par excellence* the most accurate historian on the British side, could falsify history by closing an account of this action as follows: "The German troops, in consequence of their position the leaving of which was not considered advisable, *did not take a great part in this engagement*. After the beginning of this action, Gen. Phillips made his way through the dense woods, a proceeding that was of great advantage."

And in still further confirmation of the substantial aid given to the British at a very critical time, I received just after penning the above paragraph, a letter from my friend Mr. Jno. J. Dalgleish, F. S. A.

I now replaced my ammunition from that of the English wagons at the foot of the hill. The loss of the Royal Artillery in to-day's action was

of Edinburgh, Scotland, enclosing an extract from a MS. Journal kept by his Grandfather, Lieut. John Dalgleish of the 21st Regiment, during the campaign of Burgoyne. Speaking of the writer of this *Journal*, Mr. Dalgleish says:

" My Grandfather who had previously been in the old Scotch Brigade in Holland, left that service finding there was neither work to do nor promotion to be had by that time in that once famous corps, and joined in 1776, the 21st North British Fuzileers of the British Army and had the misfortune to be one of those who surrendered with Burgoyne on 18 Oct., 1777. I was always aware that he had served in America, but my Father who was a reticent man never used to refer to the subject, and I had not unfortunately during his life the curiosity to speak with him, on the subject. (My Grandfather died—in 1829—before my birth, after attaining the command of his regiment in which he served in the West Indies, and from which retired in 1797.) My grandfather's military servant, who had followed him from the Dutch Brigade was killed on 19 Sept., 1777 in the battle."

EXTRACT FROM LIEUT. DALGLEISH'S JOURNAL.

" Arrived at Quebec the 8th of June and landed a day or two afterwards: remained there doing garrison duty along with the other additional companies until the 12th of August when we were ordered to march to join the army. After a long march, with a sailing over the lakes, we joined the army under the command of Lt. Gen. Burgoyne the 3d September at Fort Edward, remained 8 or 10 days, came up with the enemy the 19th instant at Freeman's Farm. Our picket engaged the above till one

o'clock and were repulsed upon [which?] the advanced corps went up and beat the E of the ground: about 2 [o'clock] the 21st and 62d Regts., were ordered up as the enemy had got a reinforcement and had returned to the charge. Sometime afterwards the 20th Regt. was ordered in (mistake) up to support the two former. The engagement continued very hot until about sunset when the Germans came up, upon which the enemy were glad to get off in the dusk in evening and left us masters of the field of battle: next day part encamped on the above mentioned ground and the other on the left of that. Remained there until on the 8th of October [*Sic.* The Battle was on the 7th] a strong party was sent out to try if a hill [The hill or ridge from the top of which Morgan rushed down with his men and flanked the troops of Gen. Fraser and Lord Balcarras. See Stone's *Burgoyne's Campaign.*] to our right and south could not command the enemy's camp We were obliged to retire into our camp again. Began our retreat same night and came to the rising grounds round the Hospital where remained all next day. There were several shots exchanged on both sides. 9th. at night continued our retreat to Saratoga. 11th. Entrenched ourselves there. A convention proposed on 15th or 16th and agreed to the 17th same month and signed by both parties, *i. e.*, by Gen. Burgoyne and Mr. Gates the Genl. We began our march the 18th, for Cambridge and arrived there 18th of November. Sept 2d (1778) still in this situation and ordered to Rutland: arrived here [there?] the 4th instant. Nov. 11, 1778 was ordered to march for Charlottesville in Virginia a march of 600

very severe. One, Capt. Johns, was mortally wounded and died the next morning.

Brigade Major, Capt. Bloomfield, received a shot through the cheek under the tongue.[2] Nearly all the rest of Gen. Phillip's adjutants were wounded; also some of Gen. Burgoyne's adjutants. Over thirty men of the Royal Artillery are either dead or wounded (among them not one under 10 inches,[3]) all of them fine looking men. A number of them, also, died on the field of battle, who measured 11 to 12 inches. Some are still alive; others dead.

I am the only one in the detachment, of all my fellow officers, who was so fortunate as not even to have a horse either killed or wounded —

miles. We arrived here at Charlottesville (in Albemarle county) the Jan. 1779. Remained there until the 23 Nov., 1780, when we marched into Maryland and that day several of the officers [a word illegible] they were exchanged, of which .appy number I was one and arrived safe 1 New York the 16th December, 780."

The following was found among the papers of the writer of the above by his grandson :

"I do certify that Lieutenant Dalgleish of the 21st Regt., was regularly Exchanged for Lieutenant Joshua Branard of the Connecticut Militia at New York the 3d day of November 1780.

(Signed)
Jos. Loring.
" Com. Genl. Prisrs.
"To whom it may concern."

[1] Jones, Pausch's old friend. See note on page 79.

[2] Mrs. Riedesel thus speaks of Bloomfield's wound : " I undertook the care of Major Bloomfield, Adj. of Gen. Phillips, through both of whose cheeks a small musket ball had passed, shattering his teeth and grazing his tongue. He could hold nothing whatever in his mouth. The matter from the wound almost choked him, and he was unable to take any other nourishment, except a little broth. We had Rhine wine. I gave him a bottle of it, in hopes that the acidity of the wine would cleanse his wound. He kept some continually in his mouth; and that alone acted so beneficially that he became cured, and I again acquired one more friend. Thus, in the midst of my hours of my care and suffering, I derived a joyful satisfaction which made me very happy." For a sketch of Bloomfield see note ante.

[3] i.e. 5 feet, 10 inches.

to say nothing of not having a man wounded, and only a trifling loss of a few knapsacks containing some small articles of clothing.

The losses on our side are very considerable, for the reason that the enemy, during the whole engagement which lasted half an hour, continually brought up fresh brigades, and thus had a constant supply of fresh men. The enemy are reported to have numbered from 8 to 9,000 men. It was impossible to discover the enemy's losses on the battle-field, as each retiring brigade is said to have taken with it, its dead and wounded. An exception to this, however, was the last one on the field. This brigade could not be relieved, and, consequently, was obliged to leave its dead and wounded in the woods in front of our right wing. Our small party of Indians had a fine time the next morning in plundering and (according to their wretched custom) scalping them.

With the approaching night, we received orders to fall back and camp in a piece of woods in our rear, near a road which leads from the Hudson to Freeman's house and farm, where to-day's engagement took place.[1] I was to encamp between the 9th and 21st Regiments. The whole army bivouacked; and as I passed the place where Gen. Phillips was stationed, he de-

---

[1] The locality thus designated yet retains the name of "Freeman's Farm," and is owned and occupied (1886) by a farmer of the name of William Esmond.

sired to know what artillery brigade was going by? I replied that it was a detachment of my own; whereupon I immediately received his compliments, together with expressions of his personal satisfaction in regard to the action of to-day.

Gen. Adj. Capt. Clark,[1] received similar assurances from his Excellency, Gen. Burgoyne, the same evening; and the following morning, I received, through Gen. von Riedesel, the same marks of satisfaction, in regard to myself and men, from Gen. Burgoyne. This I faithfully communicated to my detachment, announcing it to the oldest and the youngest.

I cannot pass unnoticed the excellent and intrepid courage, as well as the indefatigable labor of the two artillerymen Hausmann and Müller; also a wagon-master Ziglamm. The latter, although it was not his duty, not only stood the fire without flinching, but helped to unload the carts, which stood fifteen paces in the rear, that there might be no lack of ammunition. Under a shower of bullets he reconnoitred the road on our march up the hill; and, as the cannon had to be drawn mostly by men, he continually sought for opportunities where horses could be used to advantage. The only one who lagged behind,

---

[1] Sir Francis Clerke. This mistake probably arose from the fact that the English pronounce the name Clerke as if written *Clark*. He was killed in the action of the 7th Oct.

was the celebrated wagon army surgeon, and, perhaps, formerly mountebank and charletan, Unger — I suppose he has been all this ere now; for he has constantly "your Excellency," "Your Grace, etc., etc., on his tongue. He is a "bad egg"— such as could scarcely be again found in the whole Roman empire. He discovered a safe place and stayed behind with his bundles of bandages and lint. He also found a drum, and, in company with some English drummers, got as drunk as a beast.

The position, so dearly bought, was occupied according to command. Every body remained under arms during the night, but not another shot was heard.[1]

20th. The next morning all the wounded were carried from the battle-field on provision and Infantry ammunition wagons, past us to a hospital on the Hudson, consisting of tents and former stables. I wish they had been taken by some other route; for it is an unpleasant sight for all soldiers, causing, as it does, reflection, and awakening in them timidity and even fear of the future.[2] There are daily about twenty or more deaths.

---

[1] "The British and German troops bivouacked on the battle-field, the Brunswickers composing in part the right wing. It was a silent night. No other sounds were heard, except the groaning and sighing of the wounded, and the challenging of the sentries." *The German Auxiliary troops in America.*

[2] It is to this same incident, undoubtedly that Anburey refers, when, in speaking of affairs in the British camp

The dead were buried on the field of battle, instead of on the hill, because breast-works were thrown up there.[1] Our good and earnest army-surgeon, Heidelbach, (whom Counsellor Schultze recommended to the service of our Prince and for which we cannot be too grateful) came early this morning to me, kindly hoping to be of assistance to our wounded if we had any. But thanks be to God, I had not one man with the least complaint. From here he went to the battle-field, where the last massacre had taken place. On his return, he told me that behind the enclosure to the right he had seen over fifty dead bodies, but was prevented from going further by a fellow whom he saw leveling a gun at him. He thought it best, therefore, to leave. Shortly after, a few Englishmen and Germans came over to my quarters, who stated that they had counted about 250 dead and living, but badly wounded, enemies. They, however were

---

just after the action of the 19th, he says: "This friendly office to the dead, though it greatly affects the feelings, was nothing to the scene in bringing in the wounded: the one were past all pain, the other in the most excruciating torments, sending forth dreadful groans. They had remained out all night, and from the loss of blood and want of nourishment, were upon the point of expiring with faintness; some of them begged they might lay and die, others again were insensible; some upon the least movement were put in the most horrid tortures, all had near a mile to be conveyed to the hospitals; others at their last gasp, who for want of our timely assistance must have inevitably expired. These poor creatures, perishing with cold, and weltering in their blood, displayed such a scene, it must be a heart of adamant that could not be affected by it, even to a degree of weakness."

[1] The dead were not all buried, since, as we are told by Anburey who was there, the first two nights after the action were rendered hideous by the howls of large packs of wolves that were attracted by the unburied bodies of the slain.

unable to go farther having been several times shot at.

This afternoon, the whole army is to turn out in a body. In consequence of an order I received, I sought the left wing of the German Division, where I found Lieut. Dufais encamped with two other cannon, which were silent during yesterday's action. I now posted my brigade according to my best judgment on this mount, and then encamped with the entire company on a line close behind my two cannon. My brigade consists, at present, of only two 6 pounders under my command on the left wing of the army. Two more 6 pounders are detailed for the use of the Brunswick Grenadier Battalion von Breymann, which, with the Chasseur Battalion and the company of Yägers (that is, what is left of it) under command of Lieut. Gen. von Breymann covers the right flank of the army and is called the " corps Breymann." We are now encamped on Freeman's Farm near Stillwater. At Stillwater stands the hostile army consisting, it is said, of 12,000 men in an entrenched camp fenced in by an abattis, and occupying a very advantageous and strong position.[2] The right

---

[1] The traces of Breymann's intrenchments are yet to be seen very plainly. They lie about twenty rods north-west of Mr. Esmond's farm-house. The place is a rocky mound, considerably elevated by nature, and is known by the farmers in the vicinity as "Burgoyne's Hill." This however, is a misnomer. Properly, it is BREYMANN'S HILL. It was at the north-west corner of this eminence that Arnold was wounded in the action of Oct. 7th.

[2] Selected and fortified by Kosciusko.

wing, resting on a mountain, has the Hudson for an *appagement*, and is thus protected by it. The adjacent, though not large plain, and also the road to Albany, are defended by strong detachments as far as the river. In the thickets, in the overgrown gorges, and in the ravines at the foot of the mountain, are also strong detachments which compose their pickets and sentinels. By means of these pickets and sentinels they throw out their outposts, as it were, in a line, and from which, also, they send out their patrols. One can see nothing of their camp or entrenchments owing to the dense forests which hide them. The left wing of the enemy, according to report, reaches far beyond our right wing and outnumbers it. They are said to be encamped behind thick woods in an abattis and a fortified camp. It is also said that every day and every hour their numbers are augmented by the arrival of militia from the adjoining provinces. According to the statements of deserters, they number over 12,000.

The left wing of our army, under Gen. Riedesel, rests on a mountain opposite the right wing of the enemy, and is also in a forest. My four 6 pounders, to the left but on the side of the hill, are there for the protection of Capt. Schachten of the Grenadier Company of the Hesse-Hanau Regiment. Contiguous to the left wing of the army one officer and fifty men

of the Regiment Hanau are stationed close to
the Hudson on the plain, in front of a bridge on
the road to Albany behind a little *Tete de pont.*
Five to six hundred paces further on and in front
of a house, a subaltern and ten men are likewise stationed. This forms, as it were, a chain
from our pickets to the Hudson.

Behind our left wing, down on the plain
[which borders the river] stands the Park of our
heavy Artillery, our ammunition, provision and
baggage train, and our hospital and batteaux,
together with a few companies of the 47th Eng.
Reg. — partly in a fortified camp, partly not.

Between our left wing and the enemy's right
are a swamp and a very deep ravine, covered
with heavy bushes and trees, which begins at my
post (where are the Regiments Rhetz, Specht
and Riedesel), and extends to a point where the
ravine is not so deep; and thence to an eminence,
thus surrounding a few English regiments, towards the right. Our army is thus encamped
according to the natural formation of the land.
Farther to the right, and across a valley or
ravine which divides our line, begins the English
camp. This extends farther to the right, in
front of a piece of woods, and through a large
field of Indian corn to Freeman's house. On the
height occupied on the 19th of Sept., Brig. Gen.
Fraser is encamped, who, with the English
Grenadiers and the Light Infantry, forms the

right wing. At a pretty fair distance from Fraser is stationed Lieut. Col. von Breymann with his Battalion of Grenadiers, the Battalion of Barner, and the company of Yägers in front of whom are encamped the Indian, Canadian and Albanian volunteers who have their outposts in front of the whole of this part of the line.[1]

Altogether, including English and Germans, our army (*prima plana*) numbers 5,000 men, exclusive of the few Indians (the most of whom strayed away and returned to their huts), and exclusive, also, of the garrisons left at Carillon, St. John, Chambly, Montreal and the whole of Canada. These garrisons number at the most 4,000 men.

21st. There was an alarm this morning among the men who were chopping trees in the woods for the purpose both of making a clearing in front of the army, and of opening up a communication between the pickets and outposts. It is very evident that we are exceedingly near the enmy's camp, for we can hear their drums distinctly. To-day they fired salutes of thirteen to fourteen guns, and we could repeatedly hear their joyful exclamation " Hurrah! Hurrah!!" The cause of their celebrating this festival is at present unknown to us.

---

[1] The Albanians, however, did not reach Burgoyne until two days later, the 22d Sept. — See *Gen. Riedesel*, vol. I page 154.

The position of our left wing was finished to-day, and the tents were properly pitched — a sure indication that henceforth our march will be slower, and that a very hot day [a battle] may be expected.

This night a bridge was built with our batteaux across the Hudson; and on the opposite bank a beginning was made on a *Tete de Pont*.[1]

22d This morning, the pickets of the Regiment Riedesel brought in a prisoner who stated that the firing of yesterday in their camp was caused by a report that the Americans had retaken Carillon.[2] *N. B.* This can be nothing but a lie.

---

[1] Anbury in his travels, in his picture of the burial of Gen. Fraser, gives a very fine view of this *Tete de Pont* mentioned by Pausch. The reader will find in *Lossing's Field Book of the American Revolution*, a reduced copy of this print.

[2] The origin of this report was the successful raid by Lt. Col. Brown, who four days previously, on the 18th, had surprised the outposts of Ticonderoga [Carillon], set free 100 American prisoners, captured four companies of Regulars, a quantity of stores and cannon, and destroyed a large quantity of boats and an armed sloop.

I am enabled to throw new light upon this raid of Col. Brown, at least from a British stand-point, by the courtesy of Mr. J. H. Durham of Cape Vincent, N. Y., who has sent me the following letter — the original of which he owns and which is now for the first time printed. Mr. Durham "writes that the party to whom this letter was addressed was a clerk of Col. Christie, Quarter Master Genl to his Majesty's forces in America, but, who, not liking the military work became a trader's clerk at Niagara. The writer of the letter, came over in the same vessel with Goring. I have the original orders of Col. Christie assigning both men to vessels."

The letter is as follows:

CARLETON ISLAND, *March 24th, 1779.*

SIR: Very agreeably I received your letter dated Dec. 1st, which did afford me great satisfaction to hear of your agreeable situation. About a month before I left you I was made a Master Surveyor at the pay of 4 stg. per day and remain at that pay still.

I have surmounted many difficulties along with Gen. Burgoyen, [*sic*] but escaped being a Conventioner by being on the top of a high hill close to Tyconderoga where with 72 Artificiers I was riseing a Fortification on purpose to secure Gen. Burgoyen's retreat if he was obl'd to retreat; but the unfortunate Gen. Burgoyen never could retreat so far suppose he [had] tryed it. But [he] was surrounded;

23d. This morning, also, a man arrived here who represented himself as a messenger from

no sooner had they surrounded the British army than a detachment of 1500 of the Rebellious Crew came back to Tyconderoga to retake it. Accordingly, their first attack was upon me on top of the mount [Mount Defiance] of which they took and killed every man of us but 9 of which my brother and myself were two; after a retreat almost incredible to believe without you was to see the Precipes [precipice] and when we came to the water side our difficulty was to get over to Tyconderoga but fortunately I saw an old Battoux which we all got into but [it]

was so leaky that she was like to sink with us, but we kept bailing her out with hats and caps the best way that we could. We had no oars but the thorts [thwarts] of the boat that we paddled with. In this condition did I make Tyconderoga all tore amost to pieces. I lost all my clothes & 40 gineas [guineas] which I had in my purse which I lost in the retreate by a stump that tore my Breeches and thy [thigh]. In short I lost above 100 pounds that morning for it was about one o'clock when I was surprised. As soon as Gen. Powell saw my condition for he

TICONDEROGA IN 1777.

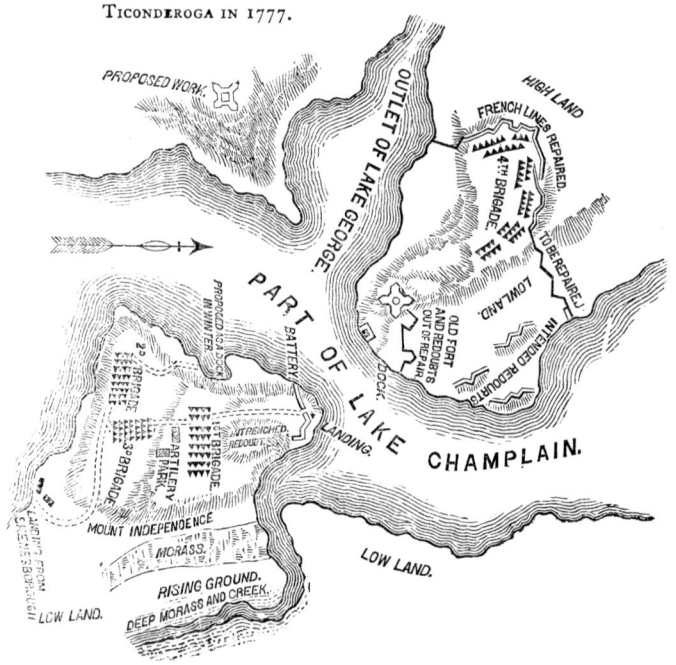

Gen. Clinton to Gen. Burgoyne. He was first taken before Gen. Riedesel, who at once sent him to the Head-quarters of Gen. Burgoyne, which was in the rear of that of Gen. Riedesel.[1]

was Commanding Officer he clothed me and all my few people that was with me as some of us was half naked as we was asleep when the Cowardly Villians surprised us. Gen. Powell commended my Conduct much in regard to my desperate Retreate and he gave me 20 more Carpenters and ordered me immediately to rise platforms that he might be enabled to mount more Cannon, and before 6 o'clock that very night I had 16 pieces of Cannon [mounted] The Rebels keeped a Constant fire on me from the woods with small Arms and wounded several of my covering party but never touched me nor any of the Carpenters. About 8 o'clock the Rebels sent in a Flagg of truse to us but Gen. Powell would not see [it] and ordered us to fire on them which we did and out of 5 killed 3, about 10 o'clock they attacked us but we always drove them off with loss of men. This way did they lay seige to us for five days, then they broke up the seige and went against Diamond Island ["Lossing's Field Book Rev.," Vol. I, p. 114] where they were totally beat, a few days after we had the news of Genl. Burgoyens Army being Prisoners and about 3 weekes after Genl. Carleton sent orders up to Genl. Powell to burn up Tyconderoga to the ground and return to Canada with his men which he did I came to St. Johns to my former station. Last Fall I came to this place along with the Commanding Engineer Lieut. Wilm. Twiss [Ib. page 134] who is my friend. I am in a very good place and have made several friends to myself by my sobriety and attention to my duty. I have keppit my health in this country very well. You wanted to know where the Bakers were, Gallowey is married, and is baker at the Isle of Oxe Noxe [*Aux Noix*] a little above St. Johns; Mahon is still at St. Johns Master baker there and both of them doing very well. Baxter is a Foreman at St. Johns and is very well; Loggan insisted upon his discharge but whether he went any further than Quebec is more than I can tell; he got his discharge a few days before I come here. This Garrison is very near finished and I may venture [to say] is the strongest post in NORTH AMERICA. I hope it will be an honor to our Engineer and a credit to the other Master Carpenters and me, and every Artificier conserned in building of it. The commanding Offir. of this place has quarrelled with every officer in this place except Mr. Baker, Capt. Anderson, and Gill the doctor, so that no officer will speak to him. I return you my hearty thanks for your usefull and generous present of Potatoes and [you may] depend if it ever lays in my power to serve you I will. I hope you will write me as soon as possible and will much oblidge your most

   Ob't Humble Serv't,
    JOHN CLUNES,
    Clerk and Foreman.

To MR. GORING.

[1] Pausch is corroborated by the *Brunswick Journal*, which states that "Burgoyne camped between the English and the German troops of Riedesel on the heights at the left wing." This statement, moreover, receives additional confirmation in the following incident. On one of my visits to the Battle-ground, I pointed out to Mr. Wilbur (on whose land we were then standing), the place designated by the Brunswick Journal as Burgoyne's head-quarters. "That,"

In the morning, between three and four o'clock, several cannon-shots were heard. It is not yet known whether they were signals made by Gen. Clinton's corps which was to arrive from Gen. Howe's army, or by Col. St. Leger's troops, who were expected to cross Lake Champlain or St. George and with whom it was expected would be our Yäger Battalion of Hanau.

24th. To-day, the *Tete de Pont*,[1] on the opposite side of the river, was completed. Everything remained quiet between the two armies. An entrenchment of newly felled trees laid on top of each other has been made. The battery for the cannon and howitzers is placed on the hill; and the openings between the trees are filled in with earth. On the outside, too, earth is thrown over them.

The unpleasant, and, in the present situation, detrimental news is confirmed, viz: that Col. St. Leger, with his light corps of expedition up the River Mohawk and its territory, had to abandon it in consequence of the superior forces of the enemy and the lack of provisions, and retreat to Oswego. We also learn that he had to recross Lake Ontario and the river St. Lawrence as far as Montreal. We look for him now

exclaimed Mr. Wilbur, "explains what I have often wondered at." He then stated that when he first plowed up that particular spot, he was accustomed to find great quantities of old gin and wine bottles, and that, until now, he had often been puzzled to know " how on earth those bottles came there!"

with great interest by way of Lakes Champlain and St. George. This will be an astonishing march. I wish to both armies great patience and pacific inclinations: for during that time[1] one army can beat the other; make prisoners in turn; and even eat each other! This news is only whispered, not spoken.

It is also surmised, that the news of this ill-fated expedition of Col. St. Leger's corps has been known here for some time past, because a small and trusted detachment from our army was sent back *incognito* to bury a small number of batteaux and to " hill " them like graves of dead soldiers, that they might not be discovered by the enemy.[2]

[1] While St. Leger is making his march.

[2] Intended for the use of Col. St. Leger. It is rather remarkable, indeed, how this singular bit of history regarding the burial of the boats is corroborated so frequently.

Upon the raising of the siege of Fort Schuyler, or Fort Stanwix, as the public always preferred calling it, St. Leger hastened with his scattered forces back to Oswego, and thence to Montreal. From that post he proceeded to Lake Champlain passing up the same to Ticonderoga for the purpose of joining the army of Burgoyne. While neither himself nor Sir John carried this intention out, some of their officers did, as will be seen by referring to *Sir John Johnson's Orderly Book*. It is, however, very certain that St. Leger fully intended to join Burgoyne. Thus Gen. Burgoyne, in a secret and confidential letter to Gen. Riedesel under date of Sept. 10, 1777, writes as follows "* * I have, my dear general, to intrust a little matter to your care during your stay at Fort Edward I desire to have two batteaux with their oars, buried as quietly as possible. It would also, be well to shovel earth upon them; and to give them still more the appearance of graves, a cross might be placed upon each hillock. All this must be done in the night, and only by trustworthy soldiers. The teamsters cannot be relied on. The use for which these batteaux are intended, is to help Lieut. Col. St. Leger in crossing the river, in case of circumstances forcing him to march without his ships. This officer has been forced by the bad conduct of the Indians, to retreat on the road to Oswego. He has however, accomplished this without loss, and is now on his march to the army. I have sent him orders as to the necessary measures of precaution he is to take upon arriving on the island at the lower end of Lake George. If he finds that the enemy

All communication between us and Forts St. George and Carillon is cut off; and our front is therefore better protected than our rear.[1] This morning the advance-guard of our non-commissioned officers of the Regiment Hanau, on the Albany road down by the Hudson, was aroused by a hostile patrol, but without any loss on either side. With this exception all was quiet on both sides.

25th. Early this morning, shortly after 2 o'clock, the above mentioned post of subalterns was again attacked by the enemy's patrol, three

are not in the vicinity of the road leading to the army, and he can keep the march of twenty-four men a secret, he is to cross the river near Fort Edward, at the same time notifying me in advance of his movement, that I may be able to facilitate it from my side. I have told him where he will find the batteaux, viz. *inside of Fort Edward.* I have given orders to Brigadier General Powell to have your reserve cross at the same time with Colonel St. Leger, and to leave those only behind that belong to the regiment of Prince Frederick."

The sequel to this burying of the batteaux is thus told by Dr. Gordon. In writing in regard to the cutting off of Burgoyne by Gen. Stark's capture of Fort Edward, he says: "The Americans who had been ordered there [Fort Edward] made a discovery, which they greatly improved. Below the fort, close in with the river, they found the appearance of a grave, with an inscription on a board; '*here lies the body of Lieutenant* ———.' They were at a loss what it should mean. On searching, they discovered three batteaux [Riedesel with his usual prudence, had, it seemed, buried *three* in-

stead of two] instead of a body. These the enemy had concealed. Having none of their own, they, by the help of them sent scouting parties across the river [the Hudson] which by falling into a track a mile and a half beyond, discouraged the enemy's parties from attempting an escape that way." Thus, Burgoyne's and Riedesel's efforts only redounded to the aid of their enemies! It was undoubtedly to this action of Riedesel in burying the batteaux that Burgoyne refers to in his "*State of the Expedition,*" when, in speaking of the reason why, after the action of the 19th of Sept., at Freeman's farm, he did not immediately retreat, he says: "The time also entitled me to expect Lieut. Col. St. Leger's corps would be arrived at Ticonderoga; and *secret* means had been long concerted to enable him to make an effort to join me with probability of success." The boats here mentioned by Pausch, however, were additional ones to these mentioned by Riedesel, and have never been found.

[1] A curious situation for an invading army!

ALBANY IN 1777.

times as strong, and driven back upon the officer's quarters. Two of our men were wounded and one was made a prisoner. It was afterwards learned from four prisoners taken by our pickets, that seven of the enemy were wounded.[1]

This incident caused us to be on the alert. It did not last long, however, the enemy retreated and all was again quiet.

There appeared at our out-posts, towards 12 o'clock at noon, two of the enemy's drummers bearing a small white flag. Brig. Maj. von Geismar was sent to meet them, to whom they gave a letter addressed to Lieut. Gen. Burgoyne from Gen. Gates, the commanding general of the hostile army. They also brought a package of letters to some of our officers — very likely from prisoners of war — after the delivery of which, they retired.

Gen. Quarter Master of the Brunswick Infantry, Capt. of Engineers, Gerlach, was sent over the bridge with an escort of about fifteen or twenty men — volunteers from this region

---

[1] These attacks were frequent. On the 1st of Oct., some American skirmishers surprised a party of English soldiers, who were digging potatoes in the *rear* of the British head-quarters *within the camp* and carried off and killed some thirty of them.

In fact, the British camp was kept in continual alarm; and officers and soldiers were constantly dressed and ready for action. One night twenty young farmers residing near the English camp and armed with fowling-pieces, marched stealthily through the woods until they were within a few yards of the enemy's advance picket-guard. They then rushed out from the bushes, the leader blowing an old tin trumpet and the men yelling. There was no time for the sentinel's hail. "Ground your arms or you are all dead men!" cried the leader. Thinking that a large force had fallen upon them the picket obeyed; and the young farmers led to the American camp over thirty British regulars.

and province. They made their way through the mountains and valleys hoping to ascertain the position of the enemy's camp, and the position of their intrenchments. Their expedition, however, was fruitless, because the woods prevented their seeing across the Hudson; and thus without discovering or seeing anything, they returned.

26th. All remains peaceable and quiet. In the evening some of our Indians returned from their hunt. They brought in with them a prisoner who although alive, yet, from fear and anguish, was half dead. They also had with them two scalps, which they had taken after their own neat fashion!

27th. Everything remained quiet all day long. Toward evening, three officers of the enemy were brought in — at least they pretended to be such, though, by their appearance, nobody would have supposed it!

The news, that was circulated a few days ago, that Washington's army was totally defeated by the troops of Gen Howe, and that the remainder were taken prisoners and scattered, is to-day [apparently] verified with much certainty in our army, but it is, nevertheless, not believed.

Extract of a Journal of the Campaign of 1777, in North America to the convention at Saratoga, where we had to surrender as Prisoners of War.

G. PAUSCH,
Captain.

Narrative of the Action of Oct. 7th, at Freeman's Farm near Stillwater on the Hudson.

Oct. 7th. In the forenoon, I received an order to have in readiness two 6 pound cannon with the requisite ammunition: also my Brigade, prepared to march immediately at a given signal. About 10 o'clock, there gathered in front of the camp and on the *Place d' Armes* of the left wing of the German troops, a division consisting of all those portions of the German regiments there represented. Altogether, these numbered about three hundred men under the leadership of Lieut. Col. Specht,[1] the commander of the Infantry regiment of Riedesel. To this latter regiment, the Regiment Hesse Hanau furnished 1 officer, 6 subalterns, 1 drummer, and 75 privates under the command of Capt. Schoel. We defiled to

[1] Pausch unquestionably means Lt. Col. *Speth*. Col. Specht, second in command of the Brunswickers to Riedesel, was Col. of the Regiment Specht, not of the Regiment Riedesel. On this point consult *Hadden* page 45, where Gen. Rogers has pointed out this error in the two names so frequently made.

the right in front of our army towards its righ wing as far as the Brigade of Brig. Gen. Fraser, where we halted. Here I found already assembled, among other regiments, the English battery of light infantry grenadiers, the Albanian and Canadian volunteers, and the small remnant of our Indians[1] who were in readiness for the march. The English Artillery furnished two howitzers, two 12 pound and four 6 pound cannon for the right wing of our battery, under Lieut. Dufais. Everything being quiet along the lines, I went, myself, with the first named two cannon of my Brigade, on this expedition.

Behind the entrenched camp of Fraser, where we halted and where we were obliged to wait for further orders, there were collected in Fraser's tent the Generals of the army. After first holding in it a council of war, the Generals went to another tent, in front of which the Savages were gathered, and announced to them (as I suppose, according to the usual Indian custom, which to me is utterly unknown and unintelligible) the order of to-day's march and the duties required of them. This conference lasted, in all, two hours, when we again resumed our march ; and the reassembled corps once more started. There were now added to the German Division the

---

[1] 180 in number; the greater portion of the Indians — displeased at the reprimand administered to them by Burgoyne for their cruelties — having gone home several weeks before this.

small remnant of the Brunswick company of Yägers consisting of about 100 men, and as many more of the Brunswick Grenadier Battalion. These latter constituted the entire force of this small corps, now reduced to about fifteen hundred men in all.

Leaving the Brunswick entrenchment on our right and finally behind us, we followed a road which led to a house and farm not far distant. This house we also left on our right, and at length reached some underbrush and bushes. Here, on the left of this road, we found an outpost composed of subalterns of the Grenadier Battalion von Breymann, which we passed. We followed the road farther for fully half an hour, during which we halted several times both for the purpose of sending out the volunteers and Indians on reconnoitering expeditions, and of making the road passable for the Artillery over the bridges. The reports of the advance-guard continuing favorable, and their repeated message, assuring us that as yet every thing was all right, we continued to march for the length of time above mentioned, [viz. half an hour] when we found ourselves in front of the extended left wing of the hostile army, of which, however, we could not see anything whatever, on account of the dense woods and the distance. Here we found a small cultivated and open field entirely surrounded by woods, and at one end of which stood a small habitation entirely deserted by its former occupants. Its roof had been converted into an observatory from which all the adjutants, engineers and Quarter-Master Generals were gazing through their glasses. Nothing, however, could be discovered. We now continued our march flanked on either side by English troops; and at the same time, our small number of Yägers, the few men composing the Chasseur Battalion, and the Grenadiers started out from one side of our line to reconnoiter.

Meanwhile, on a piece of ground somewhat elevated and commanding an advantageous and clear position, I posted my two 6 pound cannon at a distance of 24 to 26 paces from each other, and 50 paces in advance of the front, near the place where the Regiment Hanau adjoined that of Rhetz.[1]

[1] This elevated piece of ground upon which Pausch placed his two six pound cannon, is now (1886), covered by an orchard, about two rods east of the road leading from Quaker Springs to Stillwater, and twenty rods south-east of the house, now (1886), occupied by Joseph Rogers. The exact distance by measurement from Fraser's tent, which was a little in the rear of where is now Esmond's House (see preceding note) to this elevation is 230 rods, in a straight line. This measurement was made for me by my friend, Mr. E. R. Freeman, who resides near Esmond's House. By the wood road, however, which Pausch took, it is probably 30 rods further. It may, therefore, well have taken Pausch half an hour or more to reach it. By reference to the map, on opposite page, the reader may easily trace the route taken by Pausch.

Pausch was stationed on this eminence between the English and the German Grenadiers [see Burgoyne's Map in *State of the Expedition*] the English on his left and the Germans on his right. It is to this particular spot that Wilkinson refers when in describing it after the battle, he says: "The ground which had been occupied by the British Grenadiers presented a scene of complicated horror and exultation. In the square space of twelve or fifteen yards lay eighteen grenadiers in the agonies of death; and three officers were propped up against the

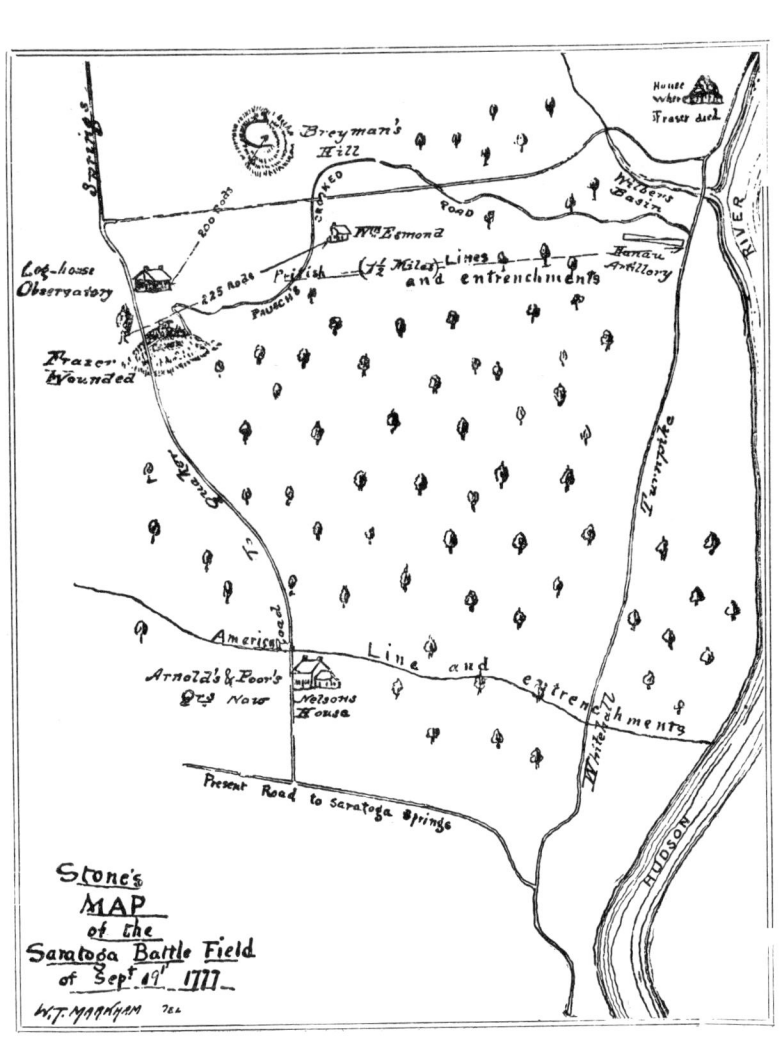

Meanwhile, work was still progressing on the entrenchments of our two wings; and it took, by the way, ¾ of an hour to march from one wing of our army to the other; during which march, not the least sign of the enemy was seen, nor were we molested by him in the least. Presently, by order of Major Williams of the English Artillery, the two 12 pound cannon were brought up and placed in front of the above named [deserted] house, and after being made ready, they were loaded. No one knew what all these arrangements meant; but I shortly afterward learned from Capt. Gen. Quarter-Master Gerlach, that it was intended to make a diversion at this point; and that the corps was for the protection of the general staff. At the same time, word was sent into the entrenchments of Breymann and Fraser, and the foragers ordered to cut down the corn-stalks yet standing in our rear. (This is called "foraging.") An English officer now arrived in haste, saying that there were no cannon on the flank of the left wing, and that I must immediately send one of mine. Against this I protested, on the ground that I had but two cannon, and in case of complying with his wish I should only be able to serve one gun; that I desired, if it was a general order to march there

stumps of trees, two of them mortally wounded, bleeding and almost speechless." It was here that Maj. Acland of the English Grenadiers was wounded. Maj. Acland when wounded, was taken to Joseph Bird's tent where his wife, after arriving in Gates's camp, nursed him. *MS* Letter from Bird R. L. Westover, of Castleton, Vt., (a descendant of Bird) to the translator

either with both of the cannon or to give up neither — one cannon being no command for a subaltern, to say nothing of a captain; and finally, that they had four 6 pound cannon of their own, of which one had but just gone past the left wing. The officer at this made himself scarce[1] and brought no other order; and I remained at the post which I had myself chosen and occupied.

After the lapse of half an hour we noticed a few patrols in the woods, and on the height to the left of the wood; and, at the same moment, the above mentioned two 12 pounders opened fire.

Shortly after this, a large number of the enemy's advance-guard, who were in the bushes, engaged our Yägers, Chasseurs, and Volunteers. The action extended all along the front, the enemy appearing in force. During this time, and while both sides were thus contending, and I was serving my cannon, there marched out of the enemy's entrenchment on their left wing, at a "double quick" and in squares, two strong columns, one towards our right, and the other towards our left wing;[2] while, at the same moment, additional forces[3] of the enemy poured down in troops to reinforce those who were

---

[1] Or with exact literalness "the officer evaporated."

[2] These "two columns" were respectively under Poor and Learned.

[3] These "additional forces" were led by Morgan and Dearborn.

already engaged with us, and advanced madly and blindly in the face of a furious fire. The attack began on the left wing with a terrific musketry fire, but, in a few minutes, the enemy repulsed it; while the cannon, sent there by the English Artillery, was captured by the enemy[1] before a single shot had been fired from them. And now, the firing from cannon and small arms began to get very brisk on our right wing.

At this junction, our left wing retreated in the greatest possible disorder, thereby causing a similar rout among our German command, which was stationed behind the fence in line of battle. They retreated — or to speak more plainly — they left their position without informing me, although I was but fifty paces in advance of them. Each man for himself, they made for the bushes. Without knowing it, I kept back the enemy for a while with my unprotected cannon loaded with shells. How long before this, the infantry had left its position, I cannot tell, but I saw a great number advance towards our now open left wing within a distance of about 300 paces. I looked back towards the position still held, as I supposed, by our German infantry, under whose protection I, too, intended to retreat — but not a man was to be seen. They had all run across the road into the field and

---

[1] It was upon one of these cannon that Col. Cilley of N. Hampshire leaped, waved his sword, and having dedicated it " to the American cause " jumped down, turned its muzzle and fired it on the British with their own ammunition.

thence into the bushes, and had taken refuge behind the trees. Their right wing was thus in front of the house, I have so often mentioned, but all was in disorder, though they still fought the enemy which continued to advance.[1] In the mean time, on our right wing,[2] there was stubborn fighting on both sides, our rear, meanwhile, being covered by a dense forest, which, just before had protected our right flank. The road by which we were to retreat lay through the woods and was already in the hands of the enemy, who accordingly intercepted us. Finding myself, therefore, finally in my first mentioned position — alone, isolated, and almost surrounded by the enemy, and with no way open but the one leading to the house where the two 12 pound cannon stood, dismounted and deserted — I had no alternative but to make my way along it with great difficulty if I did not wish to be stuck in a *damned* crooked road.[3]

After safely reaching the house under the protection of a musketry fire — which, however,

---

[1] " The brave Major Forster, with two hundred and sixty English Grenadiers, withstood an equally severe fire on the right wing." *Memoirs of Gen. Riedesel.* Vol. I, page 206.

[2] It was just at this juncture that the brave Fraser, while attempting to rally the troops, was mortally wounded by Tim Murphy, one of Morgan's sharp shooters. The precise spot where he was shot was midway between the orchard where Pausch was and Roger's House (see previous note). A bass-wood tree (a shoot from the stump of the one under which Fraser was when he was shot) marks the spot. It is also marked by a granite tablet erected under the auspices of the " Saratoga Monument Association."

[3] Pausch does not exaggerate it. The old wood road, traces of which were visible up to within twenty-five years, was almost serpentine in its course. See map on preceding page. The use here of the preposition " in "instead of " on " probably refers to the *muddiness* of the road.

owing to the bushes, was fully as dangerous to me, as if the firing came from the enemy — I presently came across a little earth-work, 18 feet long by 5 feet high.[1] This I at once made use of by posting my two cannon, one on the right, and the other on the left, and began a fire alternately with balls and with shells, without, however, being able to discriminate in favor of our men who were in the bushes; for the enemy, without troubling them, charged savagely upon my cannon, hoping to dismount and silence them. But in this attempt, they twice failed, being frustrated each time by the firing of my shells. The two above mentioned 12 pound cannon — in serving which, Major Williams, Lieut. York,[2] and several subaltern officers and artillery-men had either been captured or killed—stood, where I took up this second position, as it were dead and deserted.

A brave English Lieutenant of Artillery, by the name of Schmidt [Smith[3]] and a sergeant were

---

[1] This little earth-work, which had been put up for Burgoyne's advanced pickets while encamped between the 19th of Sept. and the 7th Oct., can plainly be seen in the map of this action in the *State of the Expedition.*

[2] John H. York, who in 1771, was a 2d Lieut. in the Battalion of the Royal Artilery, was stationed in America as early as 1772 and 1773. When he went to Canada is not known, though he was there under Carleton in 1776, since a Brigade order by Maj. Gen. Phillips (given in *Hadden's Orderly Book*) dated 14th June, of that year, says: " The two pieces of cannon under Lieuts. Smith and Yorke are to be put under the command of Captain Mi'chelson," etc. He became, says Gen. Rogers, a Col. in the Artillery July 20th, 1804, and was drowned on the coast of Brazil, Nov. 1st, 1805.

[3] Wm. P. Smith here so highly praised, was commissioned a 2d Lieut. in the Royal Artillery in 1771. He was wounded and taken prisoner in the action of Oct. 7th, and was included in the Cambrige Parole. He became a Col. in the Artillery the same day as his fellow soldier, York, viz., July 20th, 1804; and died at Leith fort, July 23d, 1806.

the only two who were willing to serve the cannon longer. He came to me and asked me to let him have ten artillery-men and one subaltern from my detachment to serve these cannon. But it was impossible for me to grant his request, no matter how well disposed I might have been towards it. Two of my men had been shot dead; three or four were wounded; a number had straggled off, and all the Infantry detailed for that purpose, either gone to the devil or run away. Moreover, all I had left, for the serving of each cannon, were four or five men and one subaltern. A six pound cannon, also, on account of its rapidity in firing, was more effectual than a twelve pounder, with which only one-third the number of shots could be fired; and furthermore, I had no desire to silence my own cannon, which were still in my possession, and thereby contribute to raise the honors of another corps. Three wagons of ammunition were fired away by my cannon, which became so heated that it was impossible for any man to lay his hands on them. In front, and also to the right and left of my guns, I had conquered for myself and for those who were in the same *terrain*, a pretty comfortable fort. But this state of things lasted only a short time, the fire behind us coming nearer. Finally, our right wing was repulsed in our rear; its infantry, however, fortunately retreating in better order than our left wing had done.

I still could see, as far as the plain and clearing reached, the road, on which I had marched to this second position, open, and a chance, therefore, to retreat. Accordingly, myself, the artillery-man, Hausemann, and two other artillery-men, hoping to save one of the cannon, dragged it towards this road. The piece of wood on the cannon made the work for us four men very difficult and, in fact, next to impossible. Finally, a subaltern followed with the other cannon, and placed it on the carriage. We now brought up the other carriage, on which I quickly placed the remaining gun, and marched briskly along the road, hoping to meet a body of our Infantry and with them make a stand. But this hope proved delusive, and was totally dispelled; for some ran in one, and others in an another direction; and by the time that I came within gun-shot of the woods, I found the road occupied by the enemy. They came towards us on it; the bushes were full of them; they were hidden behind the trees; and bullets in plenty received us. Seeing that all was irretrievably lost, and that it was impossible to save anything, I called to my few remaining men to save themselves.[1] I myself, took refuge through [behind] a fence, in a piece of dense underbrush on the right of the road, with the last

---

[1] "The Hanau Artillery was lost by the retreat of the English Grenadiers" Me- moirs and Military Journal of Gen. Riedesel. Vol. I, page 206.

[remaining] ammunition wagon, which, with the help of a gunner, I saved with the horses. Here I met all the different nationalities of our division running pell-mell — among them Capt. Schoel, with whom there was not a single man left of the Hanau Regiment. In this confused retreat, all made for our camp and our lines. The entrenchment of Breymann was furiously assailed;[1] the camp in it set on fire and burned, and all the baggage-horses and baggage captured by the enemy. The three 6 pound cannon of my brigade of Artillery were also taken, the artillery-men, Wachler and Fintzell, killed, and artillery-man Wall (under whose command were the cannon) severely, and others slightly, wounded. The enemy occupied this entrenchment, and remained in it during the night. The approaching darkness put an end to further operations on the part of the Americans. Meanwhile, everything was in commotion, and we were all on the alert behind our entrenchments.

At first, I thought that I had lost my servant and the horses which I had brought with me and which I owned; but, luckily, the former, seeing that the action was becoming lively, rides back to the camp with my horses and baggage accompanied by the detachment of Lieut. Dufais. I was very glad to see him; and far from cen-

[1] By Gen. Arnold.

suring the happy resolution of my servant, praised it highly. I found, also, many of my runaway artillery-men in the camp, and also all those of my Infantry command who had taken early "leg-bail." It was plainly evident, that they had runaway in the early part of the engagement, from the fact that there was not one of them dead, captured or wounded.

I have suffered a great loss this morning in my company, including, also, the men who served the two cannon in the camp of Lieut. Col. von Breymann[1] when it was surprised, viz: four cannon captured, artillery-men, Wachler, Frintzell, Hausemann and Weil killed, four artillery-men, H. Müller, Paul. Hartmann and Schëffer wounded and taken, and, also, three other artillery-men, Zieuhler, Pflug, and Johannes Müller. Two drivers, Vogt and Roth were likewise captured. There were also three artillery-men slightly wounded, though not taken prisoners, viz: Lotzmann, Beeker and Fahrbach. Four 6 pounders of my Artillery Brigade and also four ammunition wagons are lost including horses, harness and the British drivers. All these belonged to the

---

[1] Lieut. Col. Heinrich Christopher Breymann, commanded the grenadier battalion sent to reinforce Carleton in the spring of 1776. In Burgoyne's campaign he commanded the German Light Brigade. He was ordered to the relief of Baum at Bennington, and much adverse criticism has been made upon his tardy advance, whereby it is asserted Baum was sacrificed. After Baum's defeat Breymann was attacked and repulsed with heavy loss, but managed to withdraw under cover of approaching darkness, himself being wounded.— *Note* in *Hadden*.

Royal Artillery, none of ours being among them with the exception of a few articles of minor importance.

The entire remnant of my Brigade consists, therefore, of only two 6 pound cannon, four ammunition wagons, three wagons with shovels, hoes, etc., and two requisition carts.

Gen. Fraser[1] and Lieut. Col. von Breymann were mortally wounded in to-day's engagement, the latter being a prisoner.[2] I also know of two captains of the Regiment Brunswick, and Ensign von Gargling of the Regiment Hanau, who are wounded. Our other losses small and great are as yet unknown, with the exception that Lieut. Col. Speth, with a few of his officers, were made prisoners at the last moment.

This much, however, is certain; that both sides have sustained heavy losses.[3]

---

[1] Fraser died in a little farm house, tenderly ministered to until the last by the Baroness Riedesel. See the *Letters* of this admirable woman for a detailed account of his death and burial.

[2] This statement of Pausch regarding the capture of Breymann, differs from that made by Max von Eelking or rather by Riedesel, since Eelking's work was founded entirely on Riedesel's memoranda. Eelking, after speaking of the attack on the Great Redoubt, says: "another body at the same time attacked the embankments of Breymann's division in front and on the left flank. The Grenadiers, comprising this corps fought bravely, but being only two hundred strong, and their commander — the chivalric Breymann *being shot dead*, they were compelled to retreat." Wilkinson, also, says, the Brunswickers fled leaving Breymann "dead on the field."

[3] The British and German troops who were killed in the battle were slightly covered with earth and brush where they fell, apparently unlamented by friend or foe. "It was not an uncommon thing," says Neilson, "after the land was cleared and began to be cultivated, to see five, ten, and even twenty human skulls piled up on different stumps about the field." I have myself, when a boy, seen human bones thickly strewn about on the ground, which had been turned out with the plow. "Near the place where Fraser fell, a hole was dug into which the bodies of forty soldiers were thrown, after being stripped of their clothing by the women of the American camp."

It was very quiet all day at the left wing of our army, with this exception, that the pickets and patrols fired on each other occasionally.[1]

After night had fully set in, everything was perfectly quiet.

I cannot sufficiently praise the exceptionally brave and gallant conduct of subaltern Moerschell and Artillery-man Housemann during the action of to-day.[2] In the deepest submission to the favor of your Highness, I feel it my duty to recommend particularly Moerschell, on account of his good conduct, ambition, correct life, and punctuality in the service.

Extract from my Journal.

G. PAUSCH.[3]

END OF CAPT. PAUSCH'S JOURNAL.

---

[1] But it was more than the occasional exchange of shots. It was quite a skirmish and took place on the river bank just before the main action began. It was this affair which gave rise to the council of Gates and his staff (see Wilkinson) called to decide whether this skirmish was a feint on the part of the British, or whether the real attack would be on the high ground to the Americans' left. The latter view which was adopted and acted upon, was, as we know, the correct one.

[2] Pausch, himself, was also a very brave officer. His company, which he commanded in person at the Battle of Bennington, suffered terribly on that occasion where, by the way, he likewise lost two of his guns in the same manner as at Saratoga.

[3] It may be interesting to those who have followed Pausch in his manœuvres during the two actions, to know what relics there are still (1886), remaining on the Saratoga battle-field to recall the stirring scenes enacted on its site. Among these may be mentioned the following— all of which I have myself verified.

First. The breastworks which surrounded Riedesel's Brunswickers, and at the south-eastern extremity of which the Hanau artillery, under Captain Pausch, was placed (enclosing an area of, perhaps, twenty acres), are yet easily traced, being still two, and, in some places, five feet high. In the center of this space, and in the midst of a dense wood, is seen the old camp-well used by this portion of Burgoyne's army. [A large portion of the British camp, after the action of the 19th, was on the *site* of that battle.]

Second. The traces of Breymann's entrenchments are yet to be seen very plainly. The place is considerably elevated by nature, and is known among the farmers in the vicinity as *Burgoyne's Hill.* Properly, it should be as mentioned in a preceding note, *Breymann's Hill.* It was at the north-east corner of this eminence that Arnold was wounded.

Third. The stump of the bass-wood tree, with another large tree grown out of its top, under which General Fraser was seated on his horse when mortally wounded by Morgan's sharp-shooter, Pat Murphy, yet stands by the side of the road.

Fourth. The house which was the headquarters of Generals Arnold, Learned, and Poor, before, during, and after the two actions, is still standing in excellent preservation.

Fifth. The barn which served as a hospital for the wounded Americans remains to mark the spot where so many gallant men suffered and died, the timbers of which are as solid as when first put in.

Sixth. The foundations and cellar of the house in which General Fraser died while being ministered to by Madam Riedesel, are yet clearly seen by the river bank.

Seventh. The "Ensign House," which received a portion of Burgoyne's wounded, together with the tall Dutch clock which ticked off the numbered minutes of the dying, still remains.

Eighth. The sleepers of the bridge which Burgoyne threw across the "great Ravine," just before he crossed it and fell n with the scouting party of Morgan on the afternoon of the 19th, are pefectly sound.

Ninth. Numerous trees, which were standing at the time of the battles, still keep in their trunks the bullets fired from the guns of Cilley's New Hampshire troops. [While at Saratoga in the summer of 1885, a farmer brought in a load of wood cut on the battle-field. One of the sticks had embedded in it twelve grape-shot].

Tenth. Not a season passes that cannon-balls, grape-shot, skeletons, stone and iron tomahawks, short carbines used by the German Yägers, and similar relics, are not plowed up by the husbandmen. Indeed, I myself, a few summers ago, picked up a gilt button of the 32d Highlanders, and a silver buckle, on the site of the bloody fight of that regiment, which Wilkinson has in mind when he writes : " In a square space of twelve or fifteen yards lay eighteen grenadiers in the agonies of death, and three officers were propped up against stumps of trees, two of them mortally wounded, bleeding and almost speechless."

Through the zealous and patriotic efforts of Mrs Ellen Hardin Walworth of Saratoga Springs—a Trustee of the Saratoga Monument Association and whose great-grandfather Col. Hardin, was in the battles — granite tablets have already been placed on several of the above mentioned historic spots on the battle-field — each of which bears appropriate inscriptions, telling the passer-by what it commemorates, together with the name of the donor.

INDEX.

ACLAND, Maj., 165
   Albanian Volunteers, 160
Albany, 146
Amazon, a frigate, 47, 48
American Volunteers, 165
Anburey, quoted, 143, 144
Anderson, Capt. 151
Andernach, 22
Anticosti Island, 58
Army smithey at St. Johns, 132
Arnheim, 26
Arnold, Gen., Sketch of, by Rogers, 85, 172, 176

BACH, Lieut., 23, 31, 40, 68, 73, 79
Baden Infantry, 2, 26
Balcarras, Lord, 139
Barner, Maj., Commander of the Brunswick Battalion of Chasseurs, 89
Barner's Light Infantry, 93

Barnes, Lieut., Dep. Quar. Mas. Gen., 129
Batiscamp, 93
Battle of Sept. 19th, 132
Battle of Oct. 7th, 139, 159
Baum, Col., 173
Baxter, a foreman, 151
Bechtell, a boatman, 26
Becker, Artillery-man, 173
Bennington, Battle of, 173, 175
Berthier Parish, 65, 89, 93, 103, 120
Bischle, cannonier, 23
Bingen, 20
Bird, Jos., 165
Bloomfield, Maj. Thos., 23, 76, 86, 140
Boetzig, Lieut. von, 89
Bonn, 23
Boston, 58
Brads, head-smith, 102, 109, 110
Breton, Cape, 56

Breton, North Cape, 57
Breymann, Lieut. Col , 145, 148, 151, 173, 174
Breymann's (Brunswick) Entrenchment, 148, 161, 172, 176
Breymann's Grenadier Battalion, 161
Breymann's (Burgoyne's) Hill, 145, 176
Bristol, 42,
British camp, 175
British Grenadiers, 162, 165, 168, 171
Brown, Col., 149
Brunswick Grenadiers, 73, 93
Brunswick Chasseurs, 137
Brunswick Infantry. 157
Brunswick, Duke of, 4, 37
Brunswick Troops, 39
Brunswick, Regiment of, 174, 175
Buckroth, 24
Bünau, Regiment of, 42
Burgoyne, Lieut. Gen., 80, 81, 115, 117, 119, 121, 123, 125, 130, 136, 137, 140, 142, 149, 151, 154
Burgoyne's Campaign, Stone's Hist. of, referred to, 133
Burgoyne's Army, 175
Butler, Dr. James A., see *Preface*

CALASH, Description of a, 70
Cambridge Parole, 17, 169
Camille Mountains, 59

Canadian Volunteers, 160
Cape-de-la-Madelain, 93
Cape Race, 51
Cape Ray, 51, 56
Carleton, Lieut. Gen., 63, 66, 82, 98, 103, 104, 113, 115, 118, 121, 124, 125, 169, 173
Carleton, a frigate, 83
Carter, Capt., 74, 75
Cassel, 18, 126
Cassel, State Library, 18
Castleton, Vt., 165
Caub, 21
Chambly, 63, 64, 89, 123, 148
Champlain Lake, 61, 62, 63, 69; Naval Battle on, 82, 85, 152, 153
Charlottesville, Va., 139
Chasseur Battalion, 162, 166
Chevalier Pfalz Artillery, 126
Chimney Point (Lake Champlain), 85
Christie, Col , 149
Cilley, Col., 167
Cilley's New Hampshire troops, 176
Cleaveland (Clieland), Adj. Samuel, 124, 127
Clerke (Clark), Adj. Gen., 142
Clinton, Gen. Henry, 151, 152
Clunes, Jos., 151
Coblentz, 21, 22
Cöln, 23

INDEX. 179

Crown-Point, 81, 85, 89
Cur-Trierische, Frontier of, 22

D ALGLEISH, John J., of Westgrange, Scotland, 138.
Dalgleish, John, grandfather of John J., participates in the battles of Saratoga, 139
Davis, A. McF., quoted, 57
DeLoup, River, 65; Parish of, 93
De Peyster, J. Watts, 138
Diamond Island, 151
Donop, Count, 43
Dort, 32
Dortrecht, 32, 34
Dufais, Col., 28, 31, 32, 35, 37, 64, 72, 83, 84, 87, 106, 109, 114, 118, 135, 145, 160, 172
Duplesse, Capt., 43
Duprès, Maj. Gen., 129
Durham, J. H., 149
Düsseldorf, 24

E ELKING, Max von, quoted, 19, 174
Electoral Palatinate, 126
Emmerich, 25
Encke, Artillery-man, 72
Engelhard, cannonier, 67
Engell, Bombadier, 84
English Artillery, 165, 166
Ensign House, The, 176
Erfurt, 23
Esmond, Wm., 141

Esmond Farm-house, 145 162

F AHRBACH, Artillery-man, 173
Fauburg de Recollects, 122,
Faucitt, Col. Wm., 4, 5, 11. 29, 31
Fischer, Henry A., see *Preface*
Fort Carillon (Ticonderoga) 102, 148, 149
Fort Edward, 154
Fort George (Lake George) 133
Fort Leith, 169
Fort St. Anna, 93
Fort Stanwix, 66, 153
Fort Ticonderoga, 102, 150, 153
Foster, Maj., 168
Foy, Adj. Gen. Edward, 103, 119
Frankfort, 20
Fraser, Gen. 139, 147, 160, 168, 174, 176
Frederick II, Hereditary Prince of Hesse-Cassel, 1, 3, 6, 11, 13, 17
Freeman's Farm, Battle of, 132, 141, 145, 154
Freeman's House, 141
Freeman, E. R., quoted, 162
Freesland, a Holland Ship, 41
Friedendorf, Capt., 134
Frintzell (misprint for Freitzel) an Artillery-man, 172, 173

GALL, Brig. Gen., 64, 67, 97, 98, 104, 109, 120
Gargling, Ensign von, 174
Gates, Gen., 139, 157
Gates, camp of, 165
Gates, council of, 175
Geismar, Col. von, 89, 136, 137, 157
George II, 11
George III, 2, 5, 11, 36
George, Lake, 153
Gerlach, Capt. and Quar. Mas. Gen., 123, 157, 165
Germaine, Lord George, 66
German, Capt. von, 89
German Grenadiers, 162
Gill, Dr., 151
Gloucester, a brig., 41
Gold-Fish, English, 56, 57
Gordon, Maj., 113
Goring, Mr., 151
Goulard, a frigate, 47, 48
Great Redoubt, The, 174
Great Ravine, The, 176
Guilderland, Fortress of, 30
Guitton, a banker, 44

HADDEN'S ORDERLY BOOK, quoted, 63, 81, 112, 169, 173
Hague, The, 27, 30, 35
Halifax, 58
Hanau, Town of, 17, 22, 29
Hanau, Fortress of, 18
Hanau, cost of Articles at, 101
Hanau ships, 34
Hanau, Regiment of, 162, 172, 174
Hanau Artillery, 171, 175
Hardin, Col. John, 176
Harow Mr., Supt. of Sailors, 78
Hartmann, cannonier, 173
Hausemann, cannonier, 142, 171, 173, 175
Heidelbach, Surgeon, 144
Helvoethuys, 36, 37
Hermann, Lieut., 75
Hesse-Cassel, Landgrave of, 4, 17
Hesse-Cassel, Town of, 17
Hesse-Hanau Artillery, 19, 52, 69, 75, 129, 130
Hesse-Hanau, Regiment of, 19, 25, 93, 98, 132, 147, 154, 159
Hessian Chasseurs, 45, 130
Hessian Grenadiers, 45
Hessian Troops, 39
Highlanders, 32d Regiment of, 176
Hoag, Mr., 133
Hoover, commander, 29
Hospital Guard (Samaritans), 118
Hotel Dieu (Montreal), 61
Houghton Lieut., a fire-master, 75
Howe, Gen., 152, 158
Hudson River, 132, 133, 141, 146, 154, 158

IBBETSON, Miss, 80
Indian Volunteers, 160

INDEX. 181

Inflexible The, a frigate, 83
Isle au Bas, 97
Isle aux Noix, 78, 81, 88, 92, 102, 123, 151
Isle d'Orleans, 97
Isle of Wight, 47, 55

JACOBS, Capt., 48
James IV, 113
Johns, Capt., 140
Jones, Capt. Thos., 79, 81
Juno, a ship, 32, 41, 51

KAISER, wagon-master, 132
Kass (Cassel), 126
Kent, Duke of, 60
Kurtzleben, Capt., 43

LA BLAND, a frigate, 62
La Cole, River, 81
La Prairie, 64, 67, 89, 128
La Savanne, 89
La Valentine, Parish of, 98
Learned, Gen., 166
Leith, Scotland, 169
Leutz, Col., 89
Leyden, 27
London, 35, 42
London Chronicle, quoted, 113
Longeuil, Seigniory of, 89, 90, 92, 127, 128, 129
Loring, Commissary Jos., 140
Lossing's Field Book, referred to, 149, 151
Lotzmann, cannonier, 173
Lowell, Edward J., Introduction by, 1–18

MAINZ, 20
Malsburg, Frederick de, 6, 16, 17
Manual, a transport frigate, 46
Marburg, Archives of, 18
Maria, a frigate, 82
Marie River, 20
Markham, W. T., 163
Marschalk, Maj. Gen., 21
Mary, Princess, daughter of George II, 1
Mary, a vessel, 63
Masquinonge, Parish of, 93
Mastriche, 65
Meredith, Hannah, 113
Meuse River, 32
Mitchelson, Capt., 74, 78
Mohawk River, 152
Moeler, Robert, see *Preface*
Moerschell, a Subaltern, 175
Money, Quar. Mas. Gen., 90, 91
Montreal, 61, 89, 90, 95, 96, 98, 99, 103, 121, 122, 128, 129, 132, 148, 152, 153
Morgan, Gen. Daniel, 134, 136
Mount Defiance (Ticonderoga), 150
Müller, H., cannonier, 142, 173
Müller, Johannes, 173
Murphy, "Pat," 168

NANTZ, cannonier, 109
Neilson, quoted, 162, 174, 175
Neuwied, 22

Newfoundland, Banks of, 51
Nicholas, Island of, 58
Nieuenheim, Count, 26
Nimwegen, 27, 30, 34
North Wessel, 24

OBERWINTER, 22, 23
Offenbach, 20
Ontario, Lake, 152
Oswego, 152, 153

PAPINEAU, Mrs. L. J. A., Letter of, 89
Paul, cannonier, 173
Pausch, Capt. George, what is known of him, 17; sets out for America with his company from Hanau, 19; has difficulties with the Custom-House officers in passing through Holland, 26-32; embarks on the Transport ship, Juno, for Quebec, 32; touches at Spithead, 39; visits and describes Portsmouth, 44-46; sets sail from the Isle of Wight for Canada under convoy, 48; falls in with an American Privateer, 50; meets with an iceburg, 55; arrives at Cape Breton, 56; catches, eats and enjoys English gold-fish, 57; reaches the Island Nicholas, 58; arrives at Quebec, 59; at Montreal, 63; at Chambly, 64; his travels in Canada,

Pausch, Capt. Geo. — con.
65, and forward; receives an order from Maj. Bloomfield, 73; describes the Naval Battle on Lake Champlain, 82; receives orders from. Gen. Philips, 87–90; supplies his men with overalls, socks, caps, mittens, etc., 93; in barracks at Montreal, 99; prepares charges against head-smith, Brads, 102–109; describes the difference between the English and German cannon drill, 108; defends his cannonier, Nantz, from the insults of English officers, and describes, with great naiveté, the character of his alleged offence, 110; takes part in a grand Review held by Burgoyne, 121; receives the thanks of Gen. Phillips for the valuable services rendered by his company, 122; receives orders from Gen. Phillips, 123-129; the English artillerists use his style of gun-wipers at the request of Carleton, Burgoyne, and Phillips, 125; describes and criticises the English style of loading and firing, and the use of a peculiar kind of wiper, 126; his account of the

INDEX. 183

Pausch, Capt. Geo. — con.
Action of Sept. 19th, 132 ;.
also, the Action of Oct
7th, 159 ; takes a stand
and places his cannon in
position, 162 ; Riedesel
pays a tribute to him, 138 ;
gets nearly "stuck in a
damned crooked road," 168;
forced to retreat with the
loss of his cannon—his men
"having either all gone to
the Devil, or run away!"
170 ; his character for
bravery, 175 ; reports to
his Prince favorably on the
conduct of several of his
men, 175.
Pearl, The, a Royal frigate, 58
Pflug, cannonier, 173
Phillips, Maj. Gen., 66, 71, 73, 80, 86, 87, 90, 93, 98, 104, 105, 107, 118, 120, 121, 122, 124, 125, 128, 130, 137, 140, 141, 169
Point au Feu, 82
Point aux Tremble, 97
Point du Lac, 93
Point Neuf, 61
Poor, Gen., 166
Portsmouth, 36, 40, 42, 46, 56
Powell, Brig. Gen., 150, 154

QUEBEC, 31, 40, 44, 58, 59, 98, 103, 118, 124, 128, 139, 151

RADEAU, The, 74, 75, 77, 81, 82
Rainsford, Col., 27, 28, 29, 30, 31, 35, 37, 130
Recollect Parish, 128
Reislin, Lieut., 135
Rhinefels, fortress of, 21, 22
Rhine River, 20, 24
Richelieu River, see St. Johns River
Rhetz, Regiment of, 93, 134, 135, 136, 162
Riedesel, Maj. Gen., 39, 49, 56, 64, 67, 68, 71, 84, 89, 103, 104, 115, 133, 134, 136, 137, 142, 146, 154
Riedesel, Military Journals of quoted, 168, 171
Riedesel, Madame, quoted, 70, 140, 174, 176
Riedesel, Regiment of, 93, 138, 159
Rogers, Gen., Horatio, quoted, 74, 75, 79, 85, 91, 103, 151, 159, 169
Rogers, Jos., 162, 168
Rogers' House, 168
Rosière, Cape, 58
Roth, a driver, 173
Royal Artillery, Battalion of, 93, 134, 135, 136, 162
Royal Troops, their disposition at Battle of Sept. 19, 133

ST ANTOINE, 66
St. Charles River, 59
St. Goar, 21, 22.

St. Helen's, Bay of, 47
St. James' Church, London, 80
St. John's, 67, 88, 89, 90, 95, 123, 132, 148
St John's River (Sorel, Chambly, Richelieu), 62, 78, 96, 123
St. Lawrence River, 59, 78, 93, 127, 152
St. Lawrence Parish, 128
St. Lawrence, Gulf of, 56
St. Leger, Col., 66, 130, 131, 152, 153, 154
St. Magdalene Islands, 57
St. Paul Island, 57
St. Peter's Bank, 51
St. Pièrre, Lake, 61, 62, 65, 93, 97
Saratoga Monument Association, 168, 176
Saratoga Springs, 176
Samaritans (name of a Hospital Guard), 118
Sartorius, Lieut., 97, 104
Schachten, Capt., 146
Schëffer, cannonier, 173
Schenken-Schanz, 25, 26, 28, 30
Schmidt (Smith), Capt. Edward, 32, 38, 52
Schmidt (Smith), Capt. Wm. P., 169
Schmidt, Paymaster, 44
Schoel, Capt., 89, 97, 159, 172
Schultz, Councillor, 144
Schutzen, Lieut., 90

Scibold, cannonier, 91
Solomons, Lieut. Gen., 25
Sorel, River, see St. John's River
Spangenburg, Lieut., 20-24, 26, 31, 40, 68, 73, 81, 87, 90-92, 97.
Spech, Col., 159, 174.
Specht, Col., 39, 41, 42, 48, 159.
Specht, Regiment of, 93.
Spithead, 39-43
Stade, 39
State of the Expedition (Burgoyne's) referred to, 162
Stedman's History criticised, 138
Stillwater, N. Y., 145, 162
Stone, Wm. L., 103; his map of Battle of Oct. 7th, 163.
Stude, an Envoy, 43
Suffolk, Earl of, 4, 14, 17
Sword's House, 133
Sword, Thos. son of the owner of "Sword's House, 133

TAYLOR, a Banker, 44
Tartar, a Royal frigate, 59
Three Rivers, Town of, 62, 64, 72, 93, 106
Tour, Lieut., 90
Trinity Church Yard, N. Y., Thos. Swords buried in, 133
Twenty-Ninth Regiment, 122
Twiss, Lieut. Wm., 151

UNGER, a mountebank, 143
    Utrecht, 27

VICTORIA, Queen, 60
    Vincent, Cape, 149
Vogel, Eugene, see *Preface*
Vogt, a driver, 173

WACHERS, Capt., 123
    Wahl, River, 28
Waldeck, Prince of, 29
Waldeck, Prince, Battalion and Regiment of, 40, 43
Waldeck, Town of, 39
Walpole, Horace, 1
Walter, cannonier, 109
Walworth, Mrs. Ellen H., 176.
Washington, Army of, 158
Weld, quoted, 70, 74, 75
Weil, cannonier, 173
West, Cape, 57
Westover, Bird R. L., 165
Wilbur's Basin, 133, 134, 154
Wilkinson, quoted, 174
Wilhelmstadt, 32, 36

William III, Count and Landgrave of Hesse-Cassel, 1, 14, 18, 19, 25, 105, 175, 176
Williams, Maj., 67, 122, 125, 165, 169.
Williamson (Williams?) Maj., 115
Wind-Mill Point (Lake Champlain), 82
Woehler (mis-printed Wachter and Wachler), a bombadier, 91, 172, 173
Wutginau, Gen. von, 21
Wutginau, Regiment of, 42

YAGER, Battalion, 145, 152, 162
York, Lieut. Jno. H., 169
Yorke, Sir Jos., 4, 27

ZIEGENHAIN, Fortress of, 18
Zieuhler, cannonier, 173
Ziglamon, a wagon-master, 142
Zons, 23, 24

ERRATA.

Page 89, 1st line, for Barness, read Barner.

Page 129, 1st line, 2d ¶, for Barmer, read Barnes.

Page 42, 1st line, 3d. ¶ for Wultgenau and Bünan, read Wutginau and Bünau.

Page 138, last line in note, after John J. Dalgleish F. S. A. add "Scot. of Westgrange, and of"

Page 144, 13th line from top, for fifty, read seventy.

Page 174, among those of Pausch's men captured read, " also Bombadier Wall.'